WRITING COMPETITIONS
– the way to win

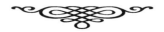

IAIN PATTISON
&
ALISON CHISHOLM

WB

First Published in Great Britain in 2001 by
The Writers Bureau Limited of
Sevendale House,
7 Dale Street,
Manchester, M1 1JB

Tel: 0161-228-2362.   Fax: 0161-228-3533.
Email: books@writersbureau.com

ISBN 1 903119 01 4

Cover design by: Essential Design
Printed and bound in Great Britain by:
Status Design & Print, Pelham Street, Bolton, BL3 3JB.

CONTENTS

1

THE LURE OF COMPETITIONS

The world is full of competitions, thousands of them. They're all around us, beckoning with alluring prizes.

Every time you pick up a magazine it gives you the chance to win a luxury car, a fabulous holiday or a lifetime's supply of jellied eels. Every time you go shopping each tin and cereal packet has details of dream contests just waiting to be won.

There are specialist contests for top artists, musicians, dancers, public speakers, photographers, rose growers, knitters, Scrabble players ... you name it!

Sometimes, it seems we've all gone competitions crazy. So it's no surprise that the writing world is alive with prize-winning opportunities too. Everywhere you look you can find information about contests for poets, journalists, playwrights, short story writers, children's story writers and songwriters. And with the Internet, you can get information on comps organised just around the corner or on the other side of the world.

The number of contests grows by the month – as do the prizes. There's never been a better time to try your hand.

So in this book we are going to open up the world of competitive writing. By looking in detail at the three most popular types of comp – short story, article and poetry – we'll show you how you can improve your chance of gaining success and winning prizes. We'll also show how a win can bring other bonuses, in addition to the prize money.

Magical history tour

Of course, there's nothing new about writing competitions. Poetry comps have been around longest. Time was when the job of poet was recognised, paid employment, and a highly sought after position. (Oh, to return to those happy days!) Back in Celtic Britain, plenty of people wanted to jump onto the bardic bandwagon, probably in the belief that composing the odd ode would be more congenial than hunting, fighting and such pursuits.

Then as now, not everyone had the knack of writing poetry. So the poets or bards organised contests where they competed against each other and showed off their skills. They did this to expose the charlatans and to exhibit their own talents into the bargain. Anyone looking for a good bard could attend the competition and select the poet whose work he preferred, and so the plum jobs went to the most accomplished poets. The great Welsh Eisteddfods continue this tradition, and are hotly contested to this day.

And story telling contests boast an impressive history too. They date back hundreds of years, to Chaucer's yarn-spinning pilgrims in the Canterbury Tales.

Perhaps the best known story telling tournament was the creative rivalry between the drinkers of the rival pubs, *The Cock* and *The Bull* in the ancient Buckinghamshire town of Stony Stratford. There, 18th century travellers stopping off in these two boisterous coaching inns would compete to see who could come up with the most outlandish and scurrilous tall tale. And in doing so they gifted us with the immortal term Cock and Bull story!

Nowadays, although poetic duties seldom feature in the "situations vacant" ads and travellers no longer vie to tell whoppers over a flagon of foaming ale, competitions still flourish. The idea of pitting your talents against everyone else's has the same appeal that fuels an athlete's desire to win a gold medal. We are competitive beings, and there are plenty of organisations out there providing you with the opportunity to compete.

Poetry contests, in particular, have mushroomed. There are more than you can count. And in Britain and America alone there are more short story and journalism competitions than there are days in the year.

It may have a foot solidly in the past but the competitions scene is alive and very much part of the present. And we predict it will be even stronger in the future. Just browse in your reference library, pick up a writers' magazine or pay a visit to your local writers' club, and you'll see what we mean.

Why compete?

Okay, why should you want to go in for a writing comp? Why should you pit your skills against others? You're a writer, after all, not a quiz show contestant or a games player.

First, and most importantly, because it's exciting and fun. You get a buzz from taking up the challenge to write something that will grab the judge's attention. And after you've posted your entry, you have that glow of anticipation waiting for the postman to call with the good news, or that little frisson of excitement every time the phone rings.

You'll soon discover that your writing life is organised and structured by the comps you are planning to enter. It's all-absorbing. You can devise a timetable to make sure you have your entries ready on time, and then build into the timetable all the preparatory stages of writing.

Competitions stretch you as a writer – offering you set subjects and forms of writing you may never have thought about before. There is always something to learn when you enter, and always something new to explore.

If you haven't discovered it yet, you'll find that there's a tremendous sense of satisfaction when you drop an entry into the post box. It's an incredible sensation when you win a prize.

If you are already an experienced writer you'll be well aware of the importance of the competition scene, and of the number of competitions around. You will recognise how significant an advantage it can give you to win a prize in a competition. All of a sudden you'll be taken seriously as a writer by all those people who saw your writing as a harmless little hobby. But beware – they won't just take you seriously, they'll expect you to buy them a drink as well!

The dash for cash

The prize may be the main draw that attracts you. Although you couldn't retire on the proceeds of even a big win, some comps offer the sort of prize money that could change your lifestyle a little. Others have more modest prizes – a few pounds or dollars, a book token, a magazine subscription – and although these would hardly change your life, winning one gives you a tremendous boost.

The fact that your work is usually judged anonymously adds to the appeal. Your work could be adjudicated alongside that of the bloke next door or alongside the efforts of a best-selling novelist. And your success, or lack of it, depends on nothing but your own words – your creation.

You have exactly the same chance of success as anyone else. Because the work is anonymous nobody can use the advantage of a recognised name or bask in the reflected glory of a previous win. Everyone's work is judged on an equal playing field.

Just a word of warning: entering competitions is addictive. The more you get the buzz from having a go and winning a prize, the more you need to enter.

The other rewards

More important than the prizes is the kudos you earn with even the most modest win. Think about it. When you're a writer, the world is full of people willing to knock you back and deflate your fragile ego. When you get some recognition in a competition, you are proving that you've not only written a piece that somebody else thinks is good – you've written a piece that stands head and shoulders over other people's best work. This goes a long way to raising the level of your self-confidence.

And never underestimate the value of self-confidence. It permeates all your writing, giving an assurance to your manuscript which smacks of success. You will even find it lends a special air to your query letters and covering letters. You know that your writing attains a high standard, and that knowledge empowers you. It also keeps you working toward success in more and bigger writing competitions.

Whatever a win does for you personally, it does a lot more for your credibility. The writing world is a small world. News of success travels, and fellow writers, editors and publishers will treat you with new respect when they learn that you're a winner. This doesn't mean editors will automatically accept everything you submit but it does mean that your name is recognised, and the editor turns to the manuscript in a positive frame of mind, knowing you are establishing a good reputation for the quality of your work.

If you are very successful in competitions, you may find yourself taking the first steps along the road to a full-time career in writing. Most career writers start small, by having occasional articles or short stories accepted, bringing out their first "slim vol" of poetry, or writing a short play for the local am-dram society. They build on these successes, establishing a reputation gradually until in a few years their work is sought after and they can give up the day job.

Even if you don't reach the dizzy heights of a career change, you can dazzle your friends and the members of your writers' circle with a stream of competition wins. And as your reputation is enhanced by successes, the peripheral benefits of the writer's life will accumulate.

You may find yourself in demand giving readings of your work and talking to writers' groups. This will open up new avenues of interest, as you'll meet some fascinating characters, and it will introduce you to a whole lot of people longing to buy your work.

If you're a poet, this can be especially valuable. It is not uncommon for 75% of a poet's sales to be generated through talks and readings, particularly if you save the best till last. Finish your reading on a powerful – or even better, hilarious – poem. The audience is wowed and rushes to buy a copy.

You may be asked to judge competitions, in which case you'll come back to this book and read it the other way round! Nothing gives you a more intriguing insight into writers' minds than adjudicating their work. And we have to admit that experience as a judge is useful for the writer's CV, and helps to reassure people that you know what you are doing. It also adds to your income – not a lot, but enough.

If you are interested in teaching creative writing, offering a personal critique service, or writing how-to articles for magazines, competition wins raise your profile. They show that you are a practising writer in the real world, and as such carry more credibility with prospective students than someone with mere academic qualifications.

Success feeds on itself. There is a pleasing cycle of wins – acceptances – invitations to undertake writing-related tasks. Before you know it, something that started as a pleasant hobby may turn into a great deal more.

Plunging into print

Now of course, this is all heady stuff, but it goes to show just how important the competition scene is for writers. At this point, we must mention that we realise many of the people reading this book will already be successful writers who simply want to pick up a few tips to give themselves an extra "edge" when entering competitions. But at the other end of the scale there are beginners for whom comps may represent their first opportunity for publication.

Often competition organisers will arrange for successful pieces to appear in magazines or on web-sites. As well as being a boost to your confidence and reputation, these can provide a route into a magazine or e-zine that you might have thought too prestigious to approach.

Sometimes the cream of literary publications – the type of magazines which usually only commission work from well-known writers – will agree to publish competition winners. You could find your prize piece appearing alongside the work of famous authors, much to the envy of your writing friends.

You can also see your work reproduced in booklet form. Many competitions compile an anthology of winning entries. In a fiercely contested competition, this means that if your work is included, it is likely to appear in a set of high quality pieces. The anthology will be distributed to all the prize winners and many of the non-winners who entered the competition.

These booklets are a wonderful keepsake, and are almost a prize in themselves. But it's only fair that we give a brief word of warning here. Most anthologies are quite cheap, well produced and represent the cream of the work in a competition. But others, unfortunately, don't. Some, although beautifully put together, are operated as a money-making scam, packed with work of dubious merit. The publisher crams in as many pieces as possible so that he can sell hundreds of volumes to those writers whose work is included – all at rip-off prices.

6

We'll talk about anthologies in detail in Chapter Eleven and offer advice on which types to go for and which to avoid.

Fame game

Your fame is not spread solely through the publication of winning entries. Organisers may occasionally send out press releases to the local papers and radio stations in your area. And if the organisers fail to do this, a quick phone call or a note through the post enables you to do it yourself. This local recognition is a good way of getting the ball rolling in the direction of giving talks and workshops.

A competition success could even help you catch the attention of an agent, either when he sees the winning work published or, on rare occasions, when he has agreed to look over a comp's winning entries.

And there are other attractions. Entering a competition gives you the chance to write a more literary or individual piece. When you are sending work off for publication, it is necessary to take into account the demands of editors. You market study the publisher's list, or the editorial requirements of the magazine or radio programme, and write something specifically designed to fit.

When you enter a competition, you write the best piece you can with latitude to develop your own ideas and try something experimental – you can ignore the mainstream and select what you consider to be the most enthralling approach.

This is a highly satisfying exercise, especially if the bulk of your writing is for magazines. In such a case, competitions offer you just about the only chance to indulge your more creative side.

Such freedom to follow your own route offers you the chance to extend the range of your writing. You can be more dark in tone, and deal with more harrowing and gritty subjects than most magazines would consider. If you usually write short stories for women's publications, entering competitions gives you the opportunity to abandon the traditional relationship or twist ending story in favour of a macabre horror story, or an atmospheric piece delving into the mind of a killer.

7

You can take risks, allowing free rein to your imagination. You can break all the genre rules. You can shock the reader, jolting his understanding, disturbing him.

You might find that an unusual experimental piece is recognised by a judge as being innovative and exciting.

Straight from the judge's mouth

One special bonus that you might not have considered is the possibility of getting professional feedback on your work. This may only happen in a limited number of competitions, but it's invaluable.

After all, a busy editor simply does not have the time to offer criticism on your work; any crumbs that he does volunteer are worth their weight in platinum. A judge who gives a few lines of reaction or, even more helpful, a carefully considered critique is providing you with an invaluable service.

This is particularly beneficial if you don't have access to any other form of criticism. But even if you are a member of a writers' club, the advice you are offered may be contradictory. The other twenty members may offer their opinions on your work, and no two of them might agree. You could be even more confused about your writing than you were when you offered it for criticism! A single adjudicator will give you one considered and authoritative reaction on which to base your revisions and amendments.

Another problem with the club's critique is that it can be coloured by the intimacy of the group. If they know that you're just getting over the flu, or your central heating's broken down, they may say nice but untrue things about your work just to cheer you up.

A competition judge does not know who you are, and can be honest and objective. His comments – whether you agree with them or not – are professional and worth listening to.

Party time!

Winning is a great excuse to have a celebratory drink – and have someone else pay for it! Many competitions have awards ceremonies, and present prizes at a special evening of readings and adjudication. If you're the star of the evening, you will have the opportunity to mingle with other successful writers and meet, perhaps, a celebrity author or showbiz personality at the event. You will certainly have the chance to wallow in your success.

That is not as indulgent as it may appear. Unless you're that rare creature, a writer who has never received a rejection, you will know all about the negative side of the business. You can work like crazy and get no rewards, no feedback and no encouragement. So when the occasion merits it, you can afford to let yourself enjoy the experience of success. It is only right that you should celebrate in full measure when your work gains recognition.

But there's still another reward you may not have thought about. Whenever you enter a competition run by a writing group or small press publisher, you are doing your bit for the promotion of writing.

Competitions are often the life blood of these organisations. They derive income from them, and gain kudos by running them. If you ever feel that you are spending too much on entry fees, grit your teeth and remember that you are helping to keep the world of writing alive and healthy.

This is not a purely altruistic activity. By helping writing groups and publishers, you are encouraging them to continue running competitions from which you will ultimately benefit. You are also ensuring the survival of the people and outlets most likely to be of assistance to you in your career as a writer.

How this book can help

Thousands and thousands of people enter writing competitions every year. The major comps can attract entries in five figures. Even the smallest, offering only token prizes, get dozens of entries.

Given the number of entries, it is not surprising that the majority of people never win prizes or even get a "commended" from the judges. In fact, comparatively few will merit a second glance. Some competitors feel that the secret of success has eluded them completely, and that they will never get the recognition they deserve.

9

There is no magic formula for success. If there were, we would be keeping it to ourselves and living off all the prizes. But there are ways of giving yourself the very best chance to earn a place on the shortlist.

This book, written by two top competition judges, reveals oodles of insider tips, plus tried and tested techniques for turning out winning work. They reveal how judges think, what they are looking for in a prize-winning entry and what is least likely to grab their attention. There's also advice on dodging the many traps that trip up unwary competitors.

We can't guarantee you absolute success or instant fame and fortune; no-one can. But we promise that if you follow all the suggestions offered, your chances will improve dramatically and the odds will be weighted in your favour. Absorb all our advice and hints, and there is no reason why you shouldn't make the shortlist every time.

And if you are already enjoying a measure of success, we'll show you how to take it further – how to give yourself that extra edge over your writing rivals.

Later in the book we'll look in detail at the three main types of writing comps – short stories, poetry and articles – and discuss their various differing requirements.

We'll take you behind the scenes at a competition and explain step by step how your writers' circle can run its own contest. We'll explain how you can make sure that the competition doesn't run at a loss, but can work as a fund-raiser. We'll even show you how to use the Internet to boost your competition success.

For openers, we are going to talk about some general hints for finding competitions and for tipping the scales in your favour.

Sorry seems to be the hardest word

There are two small apologies we want to make right at the start. First, we are using the generic "he" throughout this book. Naturally, every time you read "he" it actually implies "he **or** she" and the use of one form is purely for convenience.

Whether or not you think this is politically correct, it is technically correct – and in case you want to take issue with it, this paragraph is being written by the female half of the team.

If this offends you, please feel free to mentally substitute *she* for *he*. We won't mind.

The other thing we'd like to apologise for is that we're not giving you lists of information about forthcoming competitions. This book shows you how to find out about them and to enter them successfully, but it can't hope to be a comprehensive list of organisations running comps. There are too many to list, and they appear and disappear too rapidly and too often!

Every competition stands alone. It is organised as a single event, and if it is repeated year after year, that's a bonus. But as the situation changes almost daily, it would be ridiculous to attempt to publish a list of comps here.

But don't worry – in the next chapter we'll show you how to compile a list of competitions for yourself.

2

HUNTING DOWN A LIKELY TARGET

Okay, so we've sold you on the idea of entering lots of exciting writing competitions. You're all fired up and itching to have a go at winning cash and grabbing glory. But how do you get started? How do you find out what contests exist, when to enter them and what prizes they offer?

The good news is that it's easy. Competitions may not be advertised on prime-time television or roadside hoardings, but there are plenty of places where you can learn what contests are running and what type of material organisers are looking for. In this chapter we'll show where to look for details and how to spot a competition where new writers can shine.

Getting the knowledge

Once you start really looking, it's amazing how many places carry news and background information on comps. Where you start your search is up to you but we'd recommend looking to writing magazines as your first step.

Most have classified sections bulging with relevant adverts, and often have editorial write-ups on those contests with bigger prizes, and those featuring quirky formats or unusual themes. There are a number of great titles to choose from but *Freelance Market News* at Sevendale House, 7 Dale Street, Manchester M1 1JB has the advantage of devoting most of its pages not to general writing articles but to tightly focused, up-to-date info on competitions and magazine requirements. This is laid out in an easy to scan noticeboard format.

Writers News, at Yorkshire Post Newspapers, Box 168, Wellington Street, Leeds LS1 1RF is another good publication to study. Each issue has details on a dozen or more likely targets – more then you could hope to enter and still have your family talking to you.

Both publications also run comps for their subscribers with monthly prizes.

Small press magazines are a good source of leads too. They frequently run their own annual short story and poetry comps and are good for tightly focused "genre" news, telling you about any relevant comps in your own specialist area. This can be especially useful for more literary writers or for horror, erotica and sci-fi/fantasy fans who may feel they'd fare better in a specific genre competition, rather than a general all-comers bout.

Details of small press magazines are available by buying *The Small Press Guide* published by *Writers' Bookshop* and updated annually. It's available from most good book stores.

Many arts organisations produce a monthly or quarterly publication and these feature details of poetry comps and contests looking for short stories written in a more literary or artistic style.

The Society of Authors publishes a quarterly members' magazine called *The Author* which carries information on major competitions. It's particularly useful for more obscure comps which are limited to writers of a certain age, gender, genre or area. Membership is restricted to those with a proven track record – writers with several published articles, short stories or poems, or at least one published book to their name. If you feel you qualify contact the Society at: 84 Drayton Gardens, London SW10 9SB.

Brought to book

Of course, magazines aren't the only place to look. Both the *Writers' and Artists' Yearbook* and *The Writer's Handbook* have comprehensive information on larger, well established, more prestigious competitions such as *The Bridport International Creative Writing Competition*, the *H.E. Bates Short Story Competition* and *The Daily Telegraph/Arvon Foundation International Poetry Competition*.

They also have detailed information and contact addresses for regional arts boards and other relevant writing-connected organisations.

The *Writers' and Artists' Yearbook* is published by A & C Black and *The Writer's Handbook* is published by Macmillan. Both are updated annually.

If you fancy pitting your skills against an international field then Ultimate Media has the electronic solution. They produce *The World's Biggest Book of Writing Contests*, carrying details of 400 of the richest competitions on the planet.

This electronic book, available from www.ult-media.com is updated annually and gives a comprehensive rundown on competitions jointly worth more than $6 million in prizes. All American contests highlighted have prizes of at least $500 and all British contests mentioned have prizes of £200 or more. The top tournament it mentions has a prize of $15,000.

Subject areas covered include poetry, short stories, articles, screenplays, novels, writing for children and even song writing! The cost of downloading the book is $11.95.

Other resources

Sounds good, but what if you'd rather save your money for entry fees? Do you really need to spend lots on magazines and books?

The good news is that most large reference libraries will have a copy of the *Writers' and Artists' Yearbook* or *The Writer's Handbook* which you can consult for free. Some will have copies of the larger writing magazines as well.

It's worth taking a trip to the library anyway. Most act as information points for community events and have details of competitions being run by local businesses and writers' circles. You'll find many librarians are writers as well – or at least dream of being – and are more than happy to point you in the right direction.

Some areas have literature development officers, usually attached to the council library service, whose role is to offer moral support, advice and practical assistance to writers in their region. They are often authors or poets who are doing the job as a sideline to producing their own work, and can talk with great authority about all aspects of the writing game.

Find out if your area has one and get in touch. He or she is bound to be on the mailing list of numerous competition organisers and may even have experience as a competition judge.

Writers' circles are another great place to try, as organisers of competitions will routinely send out details to the various secretaries. So, if you are not already a member of your local group maybe it's time to consider it.

Other places to investigate? Community halls, arts centres and colleges – especially adult education colleges and those used by writers' groups in the evenings – are always worth a try. Pop along and have a look at their notice boards.

And keep an eye on your daily newspaper or the magazine you normally get. Every so often newspapers will have special one-off competitions – especially if they have a book review section which attracts a lot of advertisements from publishers. Also, many women's magazines have an annual competition – often with a summer holiday, love story or ghostly Halloween theme.

Of course, there is one major source of news about comps that we haven't mentioned yet, and that's the Internet. If you're hooked up to the worldwide web then get surfing and searching – we'll tell you how in Chapter Ten. If you aren't an Internet user then this is just the excuse to become one. Thousands of comps, right across the globe, immediately come within your grasp.

For example, electronic magazines such as *The Write-Zine* at www.gsp-online.com and *Writing World* at www.writing-world.com are packed with competition details and contact addresses. In addition, there are dozens of other fascinating websites to plunder with others coming on-line all the time.

Of course, we've been concentrating on where to track down details if you are a relative beginner. But once you've become a regular competitor you'll find tournament details actually seeking you out. These days most organisers keep a log of all entrants – with their addresses – and will do a publicity mail-shot to everyone who entered the year before. In some comps the majority of entries will come from those who took part previously.

This means that you need never look for a new competition, just keep entering the same ones that appealed to you before. But always remember to send in fresh material each year.

Making your selection

Having got some useful knowledge on the competition scene, it is time to make a few choices. Out of this bewildering treasure-trove of possibilities, which contests should you enter? There isn't time to have a go at all of them – no matter how keen you are – so which should you pick? It can be mind-numbingly confusing.

Our advice, if you are new to the game, is to ruthlessly target those comps where you will stand the best chance of success – those attracting the smallest number of entrants. These tend to be run by local writers' circles, small charities, or by fairly obscure or limited-circulation small press magazines. They usually have very modest prizes, sometimes just book tokens.

Look to these humble competitions as your novice hunting ground. They are not worth the effort for most seasoned, successful writers and that gives you a chance not only to go up against a smaller field but to compete on an even footing with inexperienced writers who are probably just as new to the game as you are.

For now, leave major money events alone. Don't go for anything that has a top prize of above $200 or £150. Cash-rich contests attract the big guns of the writing world – hard-nosed professionals and experienced amateurs. These are not the sort of people you want to tangle with straightaway. Nothing crushes a new writer's confidence more quickly.

In fact, why not forget about trying to win big money at this stage, or at least put it to the back of your mind? Don't worry about glittering cash prizes – you can grab those when you are a top player with a list of awards as long as your arm. For now, just concentrate on getting a few easy wins under your belt. Build your credibility ... and your confidence. Develop a track record.

Don't feel you are demeaning yourself by doing this. Remember that a win in a small competition is still a win, you'll have proven to yourself that you can do it, and you'll have given your rivals at the writers' group something to think about!

Start off small. Build your profile gradually. Don't worry if you don't always get first prize. Even a "highly commended" certificate is a sign that you're doing well and that your work is up to par. A writer who regularly makes the shortlist of comps will get noticed. No-one cares if the comps are modest. There's still plenty of kudos involved and hey – we all have to start somewhere, right?

But I'm not a beginner!

Now you may be thinking: that's good advice for novices but what about me? I'm an experienced writer. I've already had quite a few wins. I don't want to know how to start. I want to know how to get more wins under my belt.

Well, we'd still argue that thinking small and ignoring the "cash element" is a good idea for **everyone** who wants to impress – no matter how experienced they may be.

Trust us: when it comes to comparing battle honours no-one is going to ask you how **much** money you've won overall – but they will be keen to know how **many** comps you've been successful in. By chasing modest prizes you can rapidly build up an impressive number of wins to add to your existing total. Once you're into double figures, people will really sit up and take notice.

Other targeting tips

We'd suggest leaving high-profile, highly prestigious, national competitions alone – for now. You can always tackle those later in your career. Premier league comps attract the cream of the business – the boldest and the best.

But don't worry. There is no need to remain in relative obscurity, chasing small prizes. There are other ways to put yourself in a small field of entrants.

Another useful tip is to target competitions where the organisers have picked themes which are difficult, challenging or less obvious than usual. These testing topics will scare off many potential entrants and guarantee you'll face fewer rivals.

17

For example, any competition which asks simply for a Christmas poem or short story will be inundated with material, but one which asks for material on "the hidden face of fear" will be lucky if it attracts a tenth of the entries.

Competitions without a set theme traditionally attract the highest entry levels as writers can send in anything they like from their 'bottom drawers', so our advice is avoid these at first. Target themed comps – particularly if you're a short story writer. You may find that in the worlds of poetry and article writing – where more comps tend to be "open" – finding a themed event takes a bit more searching, but it's still a good idea.

Always pounce on any contest that asks the writer to put in that extra bit of thought and effort. Most people can't be bothered – especially if it means they are unable to submit work from their back catalogue!

Likewise, it's worth thinking laterally and considering the cost of the entry fees. Go for comps where the organisers set high entry fees but don't offer huge cash prizes to reflect this. Most competitors are on a tight budget and don't like splashing their money around. So the higher the entry fee, the fewer pieces will be submitted. It's only human nature ... and natural meanness.

And keep an eye out for any competition where the number of potential entrants is restricted by the rules. These can be limited to readers of a certain magazine, or to those new writers who have never had anything published before. The comps may have an age, gender or geographical limitation – such as being open only to those over 35 or only to women or only to those living in a specific part of the country.

Take any advantage you can get, anything that will give you an edge. Be a bit cheeky. For instance, do your homework and find out when a huge, headline-grabbing competition is running and then look for other, smaller contests operating at the same time. All the good stuff will be submitted to the big competition. Experienced writers will send in their best and brightest.

If they do enter these other smaller competitions, they'll submit their less polished material; what is left in their

18

portfolio. By keeping your best work for the smaller contest, it will stand out by comparison and you'll be more likely to impress the judge. Sneaky, eh?

Keep looking for hidden opportunities in the comps you select. Think less like an artist and more like a player. The name of the game is winning.

Aim for feedback

Of course, not everyone who enters a competition can win. And you can't win every competition you enter, no matter how talented you are or how cleverly you play the game. But what happens if you aren't winning anything – or at least not getting the level of success you think you should? How do you find out where you're going wrong?

It might be that you've just been unlucky and come up against some great opponents with marvellous material, or you've merely failed to click with the judges. But what if there's something fundamentally wrong with your work? Who is going to tell you?

The judge will know, of course, but he's not going to ring up and have a chat. So how do you get that information from him?

Well, the best way is to go for competitions which offer a critique on every entry. This is a cheap and foolproof way of getting good quality feedback. Contests either offer a free critique as part of their (usually high) entry fee, or they ask competitors to send in a small amount extra to pay to have their work appraised.

Such comps are comparatively common in the short story world and you won't have to look too hard. However, it's only fair to stress that fewer article or poetry contests offer the same feedback and assessment service, so you'll probably need to keep a special eye out for them. Always look carefully in any magazine write-ups or leaflets publicising competitions. If poetry critiques **are** offered, the organisers will see it as a big selling point and make a lot of noise about it.

What do you get?

So, if you decide to pay for an appraisal on your entry what will you be told?

In an article writing comp the critique will probably home in on such elements as:

- The reader interest and originality of the topic
- The writer's grasp of the subject
- The structure
- Whether the writer picked the most appealing angle
- Entertainment value
- The use of quotes/interview material
- Research and the selection of facts
- The impact, content and usefulness of any information sidebars used.

While in a short story competition the appraisal will examine such things as:

- Entertainment value
- Structure
- Originality
- Characterisation
- Dialogue
- Plot
- Impact of the intro
- The effectiveness of the ending, especially with a twist-ender yarn.

In poetry the appraisal will look at such things as:

- Originality of subject and/or treatment
- Thoroughness of thought and clarity of expression
- Selection of vocabulary
- Overall structure
- Use of imagery
- Where appropriate, the handling of rhyme
- Application of metre if used

- Stanza and line patterns
- Correct use of form where appropriate
- Thoroughness of revision
- Overall impact
- The X factor – that indefinable quality which makes the poem special.

All in the detail

As well as these general points, some critiques will include a few lines of specific comment by the judge on the good and bad points in your work.

This kind of information is invaluable as it offers huge insights into the strengths and weaknesses of your writing and lets you see it as others do. You can target any revision work to exactly the elements that need it most.

As anyone who has dealt with a fiction editor will tell you, getting any feedback at all about work is like pulling teeth. The best you can usually get is a grudging "not quite what I'm looking for" scribbled on a rejection slip – some help!

But a critique is a detailed medical check-up of your work. You're told precisely what ails it. And it's great value. It will probably cost only about a quarter of what a professional critiquing service would charge. In addition you know that a competition judge is supplying the feedback. It really is getting it from the horse's mouth!

Now all this sounds great, but one word of warning. Any critique which goes into detail is great. But any appraisal form which consists merely of a series of tick boxes – labelled Poor, Fair and Excellent – is much less useful.

It's one thing to know that your characterisation is rated as "fair" but it only helps in a vague, cryptic way. You really need to know what was wrong with the way your characters came across that stopped you getting a "good" rating. You need detail, explanation, guidance – specifics. You need to know what to do to make your characters more real and believable.

Likewise, with poetry you need to know exactly where and why the rhyme and metre have broken down, or how a poem of a particular type fails to adhere to the conventions of that form.

It's not enough to be told that the imagery lacks sparkle – you need to know how you could have used imagery in a better and more attention grabbing way. Similarly, it's not enough to be told that "further revision is needed". You need to know how revision could strengthen the poem to make it more concrete and more convincing.

Of course, any feedback is better than none so you may feel a tick-box appraisal is worth having but we'd suggest trying to find out in advance just how comprehensive a critique will be from the organisers.

Also, ask any writing friends or colleagues at your writers' circle if they entered that particular competition before and, if so, what they thought about the quality of feedback in the appraisal.

Anthologies

Another factor that may well influence what competition you decide to go for is whether or not the winners will be published in an anthology. Many groups bring out a volume of winning poems or stories and it can be a real buzz to see your work in a well-presented book, especially if you haven't been published before.

If appearing in an anthology appeals, target those comps that have published volumes in previous years. Buy a copy of their back numbers if you can. Organisers usually have a few left over which they sell off cheaply. It will give you an insight into the type of work that appealed to the judge, especially useful if he or she is judging again this year.

And it's worth enquiring of the organisers of other contests you're entering whether they intend to bring out a winners' booklet. You never know, they might never have considered it and you might put the idea into their heads.

Happy hunting

Well, there's certainly enough targets to aim at there! Get hunting down those comps and working out which ones will suit you best.

In the next chapter we'll tell you how to boost the odds in your favour by spotting opportunities that other comps fans overlook and reworking competition themes to come up with lively and original material.

3

BOOSTING YOUR CHANCES OF SUCCESS

You've picked the comp you want to enter. You've pin-pointed
the contest that offers you the best shot at success. What comes
next? How do you tilt the scales so that they tip in your favour?
How do you increase the odds of winning?

In this chapter we'll offer a few pointers on making the
most of your work, show you how to look at competitions like
a pro and warn how to avoid the common pitfalls that trip up
most new writers.

Here's one I prepared earlier

There are many secrets to winning competitions. Successful
competitors have their own tricks and techniques. But the one
thing they all share is a painstaking, almost fanatical, attention to detail.

They know that one sure way to increase their chances is
to prepare for each contest thoroughly. They tackle every one
like a military campaign. This preparation embraces everything from careful advance planning of their story's structure
to making sure their cheque for the entry fee is payable to the
right person. And you need to think in exactly the same way if
you want to be a winner.

Writing competitions are essentially an elimination process
and it's vital that you make sure that you get through every
heat, and are not knocked out in the early stages. This means
taking a professional attitude to your competition entries –
lavishing time, effort and care on every aspect of the material.

Don't just sit down, dash off a poem or article and then
drop it in the post box before the ink's had time to dry. Be
prepared to spend time developing your idea and coming up
with an original angle, then writing it to the best of your
ability, and revising it thoroughly.

Make sure you are organised about the housekeeping side
of your campaign – keeping a diary of competition deadlines,
preparing manuscripts just as the organiser requests them,
and satisfying all the entry requirements. Then, complete your

preparation by being methodical about keeping records. Make it your business to always know where any entry is, how it's done in the past, and what feedback you've had.

It's this meticulous preparation that counts. It creates winners – every bit as much as a writer's clever plot or a poet's dazzling imagery.

The importance of rules

A good competitor is always looking for an edge, a way of getting ahead of his rivals. But what most writers don't realise is that one of the best ways of achieving this is to make sure they follow the competition rules.

It's a sad fact of life that a worryingly high proportion of competitors are eliminated straightaway – often before their work is even read. That's because they fail to obey the rules. It happens time after time with monotonous regularity. In some competitions, as many as a third of the entries never actually get to the judge. They're weeded out as soon as they're opened.

We know of a poetry comp where 66 per cent of the entries were eliminated. That's right – two thirds! The contest asked for poetry written in **blank verse** (a strictly metrical pattern of unrhymed lines in iambic pentameters) but the majority of entrants submitted **free verse** (unrhymed lines of varying lengths with no specific beat or metrical pattern). This was in spite of the fact that a detailed article had been published in the magazine alongside the instructions for submission of material. It explained exactly what was required.

Of course, none of the offending poems was eligible for consideration, and so out they went. Whoosh! That represents an awful lot of dashed hopes, simply because the writers hadn't bothered to study the information provided.

We don't want that to happen to you, so please make sure you **always** obey **all** the rules.

No matter how you learn about a competition – by word of mouth or through a small ad in a writers' magazine – be sure to send off for the detailed entry requirements rather than submitting your story or poem "blind". Don't guess. Read the rules and make sure you understand them. They will tell you exactly which restrictions apply to that particular competition. They'll include such things as:

- **The subject or theme you must write about**. It would be useless to send the best short story in the history of literature to a competition asking for ghost stories if your masterpiece happens to be about something funny that happened down on the farm. An erudite article about the development of contemporary art will not be in the running if the competition was for an interview with a footballer.

- **Any specified style of writing**. If a poetry competition requests material in a rhymed form, your unrhymed poem will be disqualified. If a story is to be told in the first person, your third person narrative is not going to win.

- **The maximum permitted length of work**. You will be eliminated if your poem goes one line over the forty maximum, or your story has twenty words too many. This might seem harsh, but organisers have to draw the line somewhere. If the winning entry is published, you can guarantee that disgruntled losers will scour your writing for any hint of an irregularity.

- **The necessity for manuscripts to be submitted anonymously**. This does not mean you must conceal your identity from the competition organiser. If your poem wins the competition, the organiser needs to know who you are. But the organiser will keep a note of your name, address and telephone number alongside a code – usually a number – which is the only information the judge has. After the adjudication, the judge will contact the organiser, saying things like, "First prize to number 386, second prize to number 967" etc. The organiser then checks his records and says, "Ah yes. 386 is Iain Pattison, 967 is Alison Chisholm, I'll send the cheques off straightaway." (Wishful thinking!) So in most competitions, it is vital that no identifying material appears on the entry, but instead you must make sure that you supply the information in the manner specified. There may be an entry form to fill in, or you might be asked to include a separate sheet of paper with your details, or sometimes a stamped, self addressed envelope.

- **Sending the correct entry fee**. This is usually requested in the form of a cheque, although some organisers are willing to accept postage stamps in small denominations for tiny sums, or international reply coupons from overseas entrants. (If these are accepted, it is always specified on the entry form.) Be careful to fill in your cheque correctly, and ensure that you have made it out to the correct payee. You are dealing in small sums, and it is hardly worthwhile for the organiser to contact you and remind you to sign or date your cheque or to amend the name of the payee.

- **The competition deadline**. Some comps offer clear guidance, stating that entries must be postmarked by a specific date. Others simply announce a closing date, or say that entries must have arrived by that time. Late entries are seldom accepted, but you may find that a less than scrupulous competition organiser will bank your cheque while holding back your entry. Treat the postal services with caution. In a perfect world, your entry should be delivered promptly and in pristine condition; but this is an imperfect world, and items can and do go astray or get dropped into puddles. And electronic submission is not necessarily a perfect substitute. Again, items can go astray. The only way to be confident that your work will arrive is to send it in good time, well packaged, and hope for the best. But do the organiser a favour, and always resist the temptation to send your work by registered or recorded mail. This causes no end of problems for an organiser who also has a day job.

- **The correct presentation of manuscripts**. You might be asked to submit the work in duplicate, for example, or to send it in a specific font, or with non-standard spacing. There is always a reason for this. For example, if an anthology of winning entries is to be published, the fact that the organiser has requested duplicate copies means that he can go ahead with sending the entries to a print shop while the judge is still making final adjustments to the prize order or retaining the poems to write a report.

● **Sending a sae.** You might be asked to submit a stamped self addressed envelope (or envelopes) for receipt of your entry to be acknowledged or results sent. If this request is optional, you might decide to economise by not sending any. This could be false economy as it may be the only way you'll be guaranteed to receive the adjudication report, the results list and news of next year's competition.

● **Entries not being altered after submission**. You would be astounded at the number of writers who assume they can establish a niche in a competition by submitting a piece, and can then spend their leisure working out ways to improve it. If they send the new version to an inundated organiser and expect him to go through the anonymous sheets and make the substitution, they are like to receive a short – and negative – reply.

● **The correct address for submission of entries**. Check and double check before you post your work. The address you are asked to send work to may not necessarily be the same address you contacted for an entry form. And you can't assume that it will be the address where meetings of the organising writers' circle are held. Sending work to the wrong address causes delays and may prevent your work from arriving on time.

● **No correspondence being allowed**. Although it would be a useful experience to discuss your entry with the adjudicator and find out exactly what was good or bad about your work, this simply isn't possible. Don't waste time and effort composing letters seeking this information. It isn't part of the judge's remit. That is one of the reasons why it is such a good idea to seek out a competition that provides some feedback. But as a general rule, if you want criticism engage the assistance of a professional critique service.

Of course, not all of these rules apply to every competition. And sometimes contests have other rules on such points as work not being allowed if it has been published or broadcast before, or not being eligible if it's already won another contest. We'll talk about these finer points of competition etiquette in detail in the next chapter.

But one thing is clear. You must find out the rules and slavishly adhere to them. They aren't optional. You can't pick and choose which rules you like and ignore the others.

A kind-hearted organiser (almost as rare as a kind-hearted bank manager!) might uncharacteristically take pity on you and return your entry fee. But you can't count on it. And if you've submitted multiple entries – all breaking the rules – you could be considerably out of pocket with nothing to show for it but a red face.

Avoiding the last minute rush

As soon as the information about a comp lands on your desk, you should read it thoroughly. Make a note of the closing date in your diary, and also jot down your own private deadline.

If a competition closes at the end of July, for example, aim to write the first draft of your entry by the middle of June. This allows you three weeks to refine and revise, and another week to prepare correctly presented copy and submit it without having to worry about the vagaries of the postal service.

Giving yourself enough time is vital. More rules are broken in late entries than in those arriving a couple of weeks or more before the closing date. Last minute entrants seem to think about the deadline and nothing else in their rush to be included in the competition.

Before you even begin to write your entry, go through all the rules a couple of times. And keep referring to the entry form to ensure that you stick to them. Make sure that you don't forfeit your fee through some piece of carelessness.

We name the guilty men

Of course, not all rule-breakers are simply people who've left it late to enter. One bunch of miscreants, guaranteed to drive judges nuts, are the aggravating hardcore of writers who think they can do what they like. These are the kind of people who send unsuitable material to magazines with covering notes saying: *I know you've never printed anything like this before but I think it's about time you started!*

They happily assume that they are too important, too much of a talent, to be bothered with petty, inconsequential things like rules. Rules are for other people, not them ...

Another exasperating group are what we call the "copyright notice brigade".

The "brigade" is composed of people who haven't made the mental connection that putting their names at the end of the story, beside a copyright symbol and date, doesn't just protect their work against theft – it actually identifies them to the judge.

We see it all the time. People who would never dream of putting their name on the title sheet of the story, don't think twice about having it boldly displayed on the last page. They somehow reckon it won't fall foul of the "no identifying marks" rule. Crazy logic, but there you go.

Does it really matter?

Now, it's been said to us on occasions that judges are being anally retentive by insisting on enforcing comp rules so strictly. Isn't it a sign of a small mind? Haven't we got better things to worry about?

Well, frankly, no. Rules are there for a good reason – to make our job more manageable, to make judging a rapid and effective process, and to make sure everyone competes on a level playing field. But, most importantly, they're there to stop things descending into chaos.

Competitions are a logistical nightmare, even when they run smoothly. We know that if entries were allowed to be any length people wished, several competitors would send poems that were longer than Icelandic sagas or short stories longer than full blown novels.

And if all entries were permissible, irrespective of how illegible or unintelligible they were, we'd spend days, perhaps weeks, trying to decipher the worst of them. It would take months – months when competitors who'd bothered to obey the rules would be kept in an agony of suspense.

Entering the right type of material

Another way to improve your prospects is to make sure you submit the right type of material, exactly what the organisers want.

Often, when writers get this wrong it's quite blatant – the television script sent to a poetry competition or the personality interview article submitted to a short story contest.

But sometimes their wrong targeting can be more subtle. They enter work that's the right genre, but it's simply not right for the competition's target audience.

How do you make sure this doesn't happen to you? Of course, if the organisers have selected a theme, your job is made a little easier. You have some inkling of what is required, and as long as you can think around that subject in order to produce an original, fascinating piece of writing, you shouldn't go far wrong.

But even if there is no set theme, you can still get clues to what the judge is likely to be looking for.

First, read the entry form – yet again – very carefully. There may be hints to guide you in your approach. If a short story contest is being organised by a university's literary society, you can assume that a more literary style of short story is likely to win. If, on the other hand, the organisers are a commercially based writers' circle and the judge is the fiction editor of a women's magazine, the chances are that a lighter, more commercial style of short story will be chosen.

If the poetry competition is being run by a society to promote traditional poetic forms, a free verse poem is less likely to gain a prize than a sonnet.

If you fail to find any clues at all about the sort of material that's likely to win through, you have carte blanche to submit the best piece of work you can produce within the target genre. But there are still a few common sense rules that should be followed:

- Don't submit an adult short story to a competition for children's stories. It is not enough to lower the age of the protagonists and mention the odd teddy bear. A children's story needs to be crafted as such from the first hint of an idea.

- Similarly, don't send a child's short story to an adult comp. We've been told more than once: *You get so many adult stories to read, it seemed a good original idea to send in a children's story*. It may have a touch of originality, but it is not going to be a serious contender in the competition.

- You are unlikely to write a successful short story by merely reworking the contents of a dramatic monologue. You are equally unlikely to write a successful monologue by simply putting the content of a short story into the first person. They are totally different forms – each with its own unique demands, styles and approach.

- A short story competition looks for fictional entries. Your anecdotal true incidents or autobiographical observations have no place.

- A poetry competition for sonnets is not the place to air your beautifully turned limerick – and vice versa. If you enter a poetry comp with a couple of paragraphs of descriptive prose typed in lines down the page instead of as a block of text, your name will not feature among the winners.

- No matter how carefully you try to convert it, a re-vamp of any piece of writing in a different genre will show the joins.

Avoid the obvious

Of course, you need to make sure that the work you produce is relevant to the competition's theme. If you stray from the set subject, you disqualify your piece. If you stray from your own choice of theme, you weaken your writing.

But that's not enough. You have to look beyond the theme. It's vital to think laterally. You must avoid the obvious, the hackneyed and the over-familiar. Judges seek freshness and you must think how you can re-work or re-interpret the topic to give it a new spin, an original angle. Your chances increase dramatically if you can find a new direction.

It obviously makes sense to avoid the most uninspired interpretations but how do you identify what these are in order to avoid them? The easiest way to do this is to write down the first ten things that come into your mind. Then abandon them as they have probably occurred to everyone else as well.

For example, if the competition is for an article on the theme of "schooldays" your list might read:

- happiest days of your life
- having to wear the uniform from hell
- school dinners and how I survived them
- cheating in exams
- sports day
- avoiding homework
- the school play
- assembly
- crime and punishment – being called to the head's study
- the sick room

You can try a simple experiment to test this theory. When you're with a group of friends, ask them to jot down the first ten things that come into their minds in connection with schooldays. Then compare notes. Eliminate any area of the subject that was mentioned by more than one person, or that somebody had duplicated with your own list.

Remember, these hackneyed subjects may not be totally forbidden territory. If you have a hilarious account of the school

33

play, particularly if the least able member of the cast went on to become a famous actor, you can write up the reminiscences for the competition. But your entry will have to work harder than a more originally conceived piece would, because you must overcome the judge's sense of *Oh no, not this again* even before you start to wow him with your deathless prose.

Once the clichéd subject matter is out of the way, think a little more obliquely until you come up with some more varied, stimulating and unique ideas. Make another list, focussing on less familiar areas. Using the same schooldays example, you might have:

● the day someone panicked in fire drill and fell out of a window
● that glorious summer when you could only revise to the accompaniment of the top ten played at peak volume in the garden, and the neighbours complained
● the ignominy of wearing shoes with just the wrong height of heel
● turning over the top of your school skirt ten times so that it was no longer a nasty grey thing that reached your kneecaps but become a thigh hugging pelmet
● shivering on the rugby field when you'd rather be indoors writing poetry – but not daring to tell anyone.

You get the idea? All of a sudden the experiences become focussed rather than universal, unusual rather than common-place, and you have a much better chance of clicking with the judge from the first phrase of your entry.

Once you have established the best content and treatment for your theme, you can embark on the writing with confidence.

Go for fresh material

It's always a good idea to write something absolutely new for a competition and not just raid your back catalogue. Apart from the fact that it gives you a buzz, writing something new ensures that you are sustaining a regular output.

It's easy to get into the rut of calling yourself a writer while relying on half a dozen tattered manuscripts that date back over twenty years. If you are in the habit of producing a new piece at least once a month to satisfy a competition deadline, you are writing a minimum of twelve top-notch pieces a year. So even if you go through an arid spell where you fail to turn out a winner, you should have plenty of material of publishable standard available.

Replenishing your portfolio in this way is rewarding, and helps to keep your hopes alive. If you merely drag something out of the bottom drawer every time, you will find yourself slumping into a mindset that anticipates failure.

By producing new work, you're courting success. You know that everything you send out is on a fresh, first-time mission, and that makes it easier to believe you may have a winner on your hands.

Of course, when we talk about writing something specially for each competition that doesn't mean that you can't have flashes of brilliance between contests. There's nothing wrong in stockpiling newly created material in a competitions folder, just waiting for the right opportunity to use it.

Sometimes you can set out to draft a poem or story with no comp in sight and not even a particular outlet in mind, and realise part way through the writing that you have a cracking piece at your fingertips. If this is the case, don't risk rendering it ineligible for competitions by having it published. Instead, keep it carefully to one side until the right competition comes along. There will be plenty of time to get it published after it's earned you some prize money, as we'll show you in the next chapter.

Similarly, if you have a piece that you really believe is a winner and it fails to find immediate success, there's no reason to junk it. Instead, keep it in the file and try it with a few other competitions. The "nothing out of the bottom drawer" rule refers to the old chestnuts that have been lying around your study for years, not the good, original, recent work that is still looking for its first success.

Another point in favour of producing fresh material is being able to ensure the topicality of your writing. You can deal with subjects that are in the news, what concerns people here and now.

But you must know when that topicality has passed, when interest has moved on to another issue or subject. Fashionable subjects date quickly and soon seem old fashioned and quaint.

Lottery stories, the eternal triangle that hinges on the unsuspected bisexuality of one party and ghost stories about long-dead hitchhikers are definitely passé; but at one time they were the hottest property in fiction. You need to know which topics have been done to death in order to avoid them. But as a general rule, you can eliminate any work in a style that was winning competitions two years ago.

Even if you are confident in the quality of your writing, it is not a good idea to alter one of these dated stories or articles, cutting the material and grafting in some original strands of thought. The butchery will be obvious.

This is one of the few areas in writing where the word processor does the author no favours. It is too easy to run a swift "search and replace" to weed out information and feed in a few basic changes. If you want to retain the core of a good piece, you need to perform a rigorous revision programme to make sure the resurrected manuscript is a stunning piece per se, and not just a rehash of an earlier story.

Another problem with an older piece of writing is that you might have to adapt its length to suit the parameters of the current competition. Be very careful. Slashing an old piece to fit a new, shorter word limit knocks its balance. Feeding in extra material to pad a piece that is too short gives it the smooth lines of an ill-stuffed cushion.

Remember, if an old story or poem has been gathering dust for years or has done the rounds several times, it could be that it is not quite up to scratch. It is better to try out something fresh than to waste your entry money.

We warned that an old manuscript may be dealing with topics that are dated and unfashionable, but even if you are producing a new piece, it is important to think about the question of topicality. The judge will be reading entries a couple of weeks after the closing date, which in turn will be several weeks after you came up with the idea. A hot topical issue will have cooled considerably in that time.

If you want to be up to the moment, jump in on a subject as it is just emerging and with luck the judge will be reading your entry before it has become commonplace. The trick is knowing when to jump off the bandwagon – and it may be sooner than you think. After all, today's topicality is tomorrow's tedium.

Know the clichés

Whether or not you are concerned with keeping your topic up to the minute, you need to have some sensitivity for the old chestnuts of writing: those plots which you may think are new and fresh but have been covered hundreds of times before.

The last reaction you want to inspire in a judge is a deep sigh and an: *Oh no, not again.* Such topics include the story where the narrator turns out to be the character's dog, cat or anteater; the poem about seeing the light at the end of the tunnel that finishes with the birth of the baby and the article which is an essay on the prison system.

We'll be going into more detail about shop-worn themes in the chapters on short stories, poetry and articles, but the main problem for the competitor is recognising that a theme has been treated ad nauseam, sometimes to the extent where it becomes a modern urban myth.

Unfortunately there is no regularly updated list of plots to avoid – you simply have to be vigilant and hope you can identify trends in your chosen genre that indicate a huge outpouring of manuscripts on subjects which you thought were original.

Appearances count

You've finished your entry and you're about to drop it into the post box. It's so good that no judge with a scrap of intelligence could fail to give it a prize. So what does it matter that it's an altered copy, with a coffee ring on the third page and stuffed into a scruffy, torn envelope? Actually, it matters a lot.

If you have enough confidence in yourself not only to write your piece in the first place but also to pitch it against other writers' best work in a competition, you should be sufficiently professional to make sure it looks the part.

Judges are human – believe it or not – and the smart presentation of a manuscript has the same effect as the well-groomed appearance of a job candidate at an interview. A pressed suit won't guarantee that you are the most efficient accountant the firm could employ, but it shows you had enough respect for the company to bother to turn up in smart clothes. Likewise, a perfectly produced manuscript may not be the best piece submitted, but it shows that the writer had enough respect for the competition to go to a little trouble with his entry.

Before you make your final copy, check your work for any silly mistakes, such as incorrect spellings or problems with grammar, syntax or punctuation. You can put these right in an instant, so there is no need to let the judge see your error.

If you feel you have a weakness in any of these areas, check the details. Look up spellings in a dictionary and if you're such a poor speller that you don't know where to start, there is a special dictionary devised just for you, listing words by the most common mis-spellings rather than in the correctly spelt order.

Text books on grammar, including syntax and punctuation, abound. You can read weighty tomes on the subject, but we recommend the use of something simpler which gives you all the information you need in an easy-to-follow format. There are some books on grammar designed specifically for writers. Or why not look at a children's grammar book? They are clearly laid out, contain all that you need to know, and you don't have to work through great chunks of explanation to reach the bits you require.

Although simple errors will not eliminate your piece at a first reading, they can make a lot of difference in the final analysis. We know of one competition where two poems of equal merit vied for a large prize. It was impossible to choose between them – both were excellent, inspired pieces of writing. After much reading and heart-searching, the judge awarded the prize to the entry that was perfectly punctuated. The second prize went to the poem with the misplaced apostrophe.

Your word processor probably has a spelling checker – but use it with caution and never rely on it. If you have mis-typed a word but inadvertently created a correct word, it may not be spotted.

For example, if you meant to type *of* and ended up with *or*, a spell checker would not find any problem with it, but would recognise the word and let it pass. You yourself might not spot the mistake on the screen. So it is important to check the final printed version before you post it.

Just my type!

It goes without saying that the work should be typed. Even if the rules allow you to send in handwritten work, the scribbles on the paper scream "amateur" at the judge. The judge will, of course, still read your entry, but will approach it in a far less positive frame of mind.

A neatly printed, word processed document looks and feels right, but an ordinary typewriter can deliver the goods. Do check, however, that the print is clear and even. The old portable typewriters were notorious for their inability to work in straight lines, and produced a disconcertingly wobbly effect. If your typewriter uses a multi-strike ribbon, make sure you replace it frequently as thin, faded letters will not impress.

Use clean, uncreased, white A4 size paper of standard weight – 80gms photocopying paper is ideal. You can buy it cheaply from any stationery shop.

Nothing looks worse than an entry on dog-eared yellowing paper – except, perhaps, a sheet of pale pink notepaper with daisies and little hearts printed around the border. (Yes, you can buy it like that – we've seen it.) Avoid neon colours, and above all do not invest in a set of felt tips or coloured ink or gel pens with which to add an interesting border. Use a straight, standard typeface of about 12 point to make it easy on the eyes.

Resist the temptation to experiment with all the fancy forms of print on your word processor. Using a font that resembles hand writing will defeat the object of typing the material in the first place. Setting work in italics makes it difficult to read, and will give the judge a headache. It won't make him your friend.

Paper storm

Be extravagant with your paper. Okay, so it may not make sense financially or ecologically, but it is just what the judge wants to see. (And he's the one you're trying to please.) Prose competitions should by typed in double spacing, with wide margins all around the print (an inch-wide frame) and typed on one side of the paper only. Aim to have no more than 250 words to the page.

Poetry is usually presented in single spacing, with a wide left hand margin. Leave a white space between stanzas. You should be able to get about 60 lines of poetry (including spaces and titles) onto a sheet of A4. And don't centre your poem. It may look pretty on the page, but it is much more difficult for the judge to read.

Incidentally, don't make the common mistake of thinking that double spacing means hitting the space bar twice between words or between letters. The expression is short for double **line** spacing and simply means having white space between the lines of text so that the type doesn't sit immediately on top of the line below. All word processors and computers have settings for double line spacing, and typewriters can also be set to double spacing.

Don't skimp on the envelope. If you try to cram an entry into an envelope that is too small, the creases will ruin your careful presentation. Treat yourself to some new envelopes, too. Of course, the judge himself won't know if you used a scruffy, second hand envelope to submit your work, but if it has any bends or rips these will, again, mark your manuscript.

Entries that smell of smoke or perfume, that are greasy or sticky, or have food or drink on them create a bad impression. It's amazing how many writers cannot check a manuscript unless they have a cigarette in one hand and a coffee in the other – and leave the stains and scents to prove it.

If you are typing and you make a mistake, don't submit the page to the competition unless your alteration is completely undetectable. A crust of liquid paper or a mess of scribbling-out is not acceptable.

If you must submit an elderly piece to a competition, make a new copy of it, or at the very least re-print the title sheet you have used.

Remember, you only get one chance at making a good first impression!

*   *   *

Okay, that's enough on obeying the rules and making sure your presentation is perfect. We hope we have demonstrated how important it is to ensure that your entry is well put together as well as being well written.

In the next section we'll be looking at the common pitfalls that spell disaster for unwary competitors and offering top tips on working more slickly and professionally.

4

VITAL DOS AND DON'TS

By now you're starting to look more sharply and ruthlessly at the best competitions to pick, and selecting the surest methods to make your entry stand out. You could look upon the first three chapters as your "basic training" if you like, knocking you into shape as a competitor. Well, now it's time to leave the arts of reconnaissance and tactics and move on to the question of morals and ethics.

In this section we'll talk about the etiquette of competitions – the customs, conventions and courtesies that you should always observe and respect. We will also offer useful hints on developing good working practices, and look at the advantages of having a professional and responsible attitude to competing.

Why worry about etiquette?

It's a good question. Surely if you obey the printed rules, that's enough? Isn't all that olde worlde civility and good manners out of date and irrelevant? Aren't these little niceties a bit fussy, twee and tiresome?

Well, yes if we were merely going on about being polite and showing respect then you'd probably have a good point. But in the context of competitions what we're really talking about is any behaviour which – breaking the rules or not – is going to upset the judge, ruin your reputation in the writing world or land you in hot water.

It's any action by you that flouts the sportsmanlike spirit of the contest, which smacks of being devious or underhand. It's any ruse you try which means you aren't competing fairly or honestly. In other words, it's any attempt to cheat, steal or pass yourself off as something – or someone – you're not.

So, we are going to look at these misdemeanours and their consequences now. Not because we feel you should be a jolly nice fellow who always plays a straight bat and does the decent thing – but because skulduggery will inevitably cause you immense grief.

The quick way to land in trouble

So what is the worst possible breach of etiquette? What should you avoid doing at all costs?

Up there near the top of the list is submitting the same story, poem or article to two competitions simultaneously. This really angers organisers as they naturally expect all work sent to them to be offered exclusively. They want to feel you view their competition as special. They don't like the idea that you have got a huge list of likely targets and are mass-mailing photocopies of your work to all of them.

Apart from being rude, playing competitions off against each other in this way can get messy. What happens if two rival groups decide at the same time that your piece is the winner and then each publicises your success in the same writing magazine! It won't take long for your scheme to be uncovered, and then you risk being publicly and humiliatingly stripped of both prizes.

Imagine how embarrassing it would be facing your writing friends after that. Imagine the heartbreak of having to put the cheques back in envelopes and return them with grovelling apology notes!

You'd be blacklisted by both groups and find you'd acquired a lousy reputation into the bargain.

Two-timing is extremely risky (ask any office Romeo) yet people try this dodge all the time, believing they'll never be found out. But it's surprising how often they're rumbled. They forget that the world of competitions is remarkably small and close-knit, and there's a possibility that it will be the same person judging both comps.

Alison and I can relate occasions when we've uncovered simultaneous entries in competitions. Although we took pity on the offenders and didn't unmask them, we did immediately disqualify their work from both contests. But not all judges are as kind, forgiving or discreet, so beware!

Now, don't get the wrong idea here. Some competitors get a little confused and think that the rule stating work "must not be entered in any other competition" means that their piece should never have been offered anywhere else at any time.

It doesn't mean that. It just means that it shouldn't be entered concurrently in two rival contests. When one comp is safely over and the results have been announced, it's fine to send off your poem, article or short story to another contest. (Assuming, of course, that your piece hasn't won the first one.)

Some organisers make it clear by stating in their rules: *work must not be entered in any other competition **running this year***.

Second time around

Another big no-no is sending in a piece that has already won a competition elsewhere. Although some poetry competitions **are** open to work that's already snatched prize-winning success, journalism and short story comps actively frown on it.

Once again, it's easy to get caught out. The organisers of various competitions keep an eye on what their rivals are up to and will spot a piece in a winner's list that's already won somewhere else. If another competitor reads your winning effort and remembers having seen it printed somewhere before, he'll be on the phone to the organisers like a shot, complaining. Disqualification is inevitable.

Even when the printed rules do not specifically prohibit submitting previously successful work, it will likely just be an oversight by the organisers. So if you are unsure – especially with poetry comps – contact the organisers and find out.

By the way, we'll put a few minds at ease and point out that being short-listed or getting a special commendation in a previous tournament doesn't bar you. What organisers don't want to see is work that won a first, second or third prize – especially a cash prize.

The thinking behind this convention is that all competitors should have an equal chance, with no-one continually hogging the glory. If you've already won with a particular story or poem then you've had your fifteen minutes of fame and you should let someone else have their turn.

Competitions exist to promote innovation. If experienced, professional writers were allowed to enter the same handful of winning entries all the time, they'd block all new-comers and fresh talent would not be allowed to blossom. It would also get very boring for judges, seeing the same small clutch of prize-winning work coming round each time.

So please, don't try to get two bites at the cherry. Let others have a chance. If you want to repeat your success, use all the same ingredients, enthusiasm and inspiration to create a new, fresh piece of work.

And don't be fooled into believing that you can put one over on a competition's organisers by renaming your previously winning effort and entering it with a new title. Even in its repackaged form, someone will recognise it.

The same thing goes for submitting work that's already been published. Even if the rules don't specifically prohibit it, the organisers won't want you to enter it. They'd see it as giving you an unfair advantage.

The publication principle

Now, people sometimes get a little confused by exactly what's meant by "publication". Especially in this electronic age, it can be difficult to decide just when something has been officially published.

So does putting your short story on your own personal Internet website constitute publication? Is reading your poem aloud to your writers' group enough to disqualify it from being used in future competitions? What if it's already appeared in a small press magazine?

Well, it can all seem a bit confusing, but our advice is to look upon publication as the work having been reproduced in a **permanent** format. That means being printed in an anthology, book or magazine, or being issued on any type of tape or computer program.

It doesn't matter whether the publication was in your own country or abroad, it still counts. And it doesn't matter how long ago it happened. It still bars your work from competition – even if it was printed in a small press magazine that has since ceased publication or in a village newsletter that was seen by only 20 people.

When it comes to work that's been performed, the dividing line is if it has been broadcast. Most competition organisers won't mind you entering material that you've read out to an audience, but they will object to work that has been transmitted on television or radio ... even on local radio or hospital radio.

The situation with the Internet is a little more chaotic, and no-one really knows for sure what is permissable and what isn't. Some day, hopefully, someone will sort it all out. But we'd suggest that displaying your work on your own site is okay. It constitutes publication only if you'd submitted it to an e-zine which then reproduced it as part of its contents. The involvement of an editor, and any written agreement to use the work, would mean it had been technically published – even if it was later taken off the site.

By the way, it doesn't matter whether you got paid for your work or not. As most small press writers will tell you, seeing your material in print doesn't mean you've received any money for it!

Anything permanently reproduced counts – even if you didn't earn a penny. The same goes for radio. It doesn't matter whether you were paid or not, the transmission still counts as publication.

So this raises a vital point – it's especially important that you think about the prize-winning potential of any work you create before allowing it to be published or broadcast.

It would be maddening to agree to let it appear in a small press magazine (or anywhere else) where all you get is a free copy and a pat on the back, and hence immediately disqualify it from a very lucrative competition.

For this reason we always suggest entering new work in competitions **first**. When it's covered itself in glory – and cash – then is the time to offer it to editors.

Don't worry. Most magazine editors are happy to publish something that's already won a prize. They usually aren't concerned because they reckon hardly anyone will have already seen the work – even if it has appeared on a winners' website. Unless, of course, your winner has been published in a large circulation magazine as part of the prize!

Unfortunately, it doesn't work the other way. Competition adjudicators won't be happy if you enter a story that has already been published in a high-profile magazine and may have been seen by thousands of readers. There will be a real danger that the judge or the adjudicating committee may have unwittingly read it and the piece would get an unfair edge.

Your cheating heart

These aren't the only breaches of etiquette that will get you into trouble. Passing yourself off as something you're not is guaranteed to cause you severe problems.

If a tournament is open solely to writers who've never had anything published, don't be tempted to enter if you've already had success somewhere before – even if it was a long time ago, in a different genre or even in a different region or country.

Sure as eggs are eggs, your previous work will resurface and you'll be exposed. People have long memories. Someone will remember having read your material before. They always do.

And switching continents won't help. With international links on the Internet, and the information sharing of the constantly shrinking global village, your writing past in one part of the world won't remain a secret for long.

Other things to avoid are lying about your age, gender, hometown or background just to qualify for a restricted entry comp. If you win, the organisers will publicise your success. People who know you will let the cat out of the bag. You'll be disqualified – and shamed.

Think of the problems caused if you are a man and you pretend to be a woman writer. What happens when you're invited to the award ceremony? Do you feign illness? Do you confess and face the judge's wrath? Or do you struggle into your partner's clothes, don a wig, slap on make-up and turn up hoping no-one will suspect? Who knows, you might get away with it – if your legs aren't too hairy and your voice is high enough. But if you get rumbled, then it's a lifetime appearing on the Jerry Springer Show!

Joking aside, it's not worth the hassle, so don't cheat. There are plenty of competitions, more than enough to go round, so there's no need to be underhand. Only enter the ones that you are entitled to.

Stop, thief!

Possibly the worst crime any competitor can commit is that of plagiarism – stealing someone else's work and passing it off as your own. Most writers would agree that this is unforgivable and that anyone caught red handed should be soundly booted from one end of the street to the other by the judge, committee and every other competitor – plus all their families! Yet, many people have the cheek, the contempt and the lack of self-respect to try their luck with material they've lifted from somewhere else.

They think that they can pass off the lyrics of a popular song as a poem and no-one will know. They believe that they can lift the entire plot of a famous short story (usually a Roald Dahl story!) and the judge will be too stupid to spot it.

Of course, these dishonest people always get caught. The judge is then placed in the onerous position of wondering whether to quietly disqualify the thieves with a sad shake of the head, or expose the culprits.

It's not something that a judge does lightly, as it means the certain end of a writer's competitions career. Some adjudicators prefer to let things slide for the sake of a quiet life, but we're both "shouting it from the rooftops" merchants. So beware!

The thinking here is simple. If you lift someone else's work *word for word* then it's theft. If you lift it and alter a few words for camouflage, it's still theft – you're just a slightly smarter thief. You might have changed enough to escape a copyright infringement action by the original author, but you've still broken the fair-play convention of competitions. You'll have breached etiquette.

And something to bear in mind is that a competition judge isn't the same as a judge in a court of law. We don't need to worry about "the burden of proof", or "things being proved beyond a reasonable doubt". If common sense and experience make us suspect you've been light-fingered, we will disqualify you.

Neither of us understands why people plagiarise. Surely, you want to win glory for your own ingenuity and creativity – not the stickiness of your fingers!

Where the line is drawn

But what about merely being inspired by someone else's writing? Is that okay? The short answer is yes – as long as you're honest in your intentions. All writers will admit that they have been influenced at some time by the work of others.

And there's no shame in reading a short story, for example, and thinking that the characters weren't right and the ending didn't work. You give it some thought and come up with a new, dramatically-altered plot – complete with fresh characters, a different setting, your own original dialogue and descriptions, and then crown it all with a unique and novel denouement.

That's okay, the new work bears no resemblance to the original. It's merely acted as a catalyst, jump-starting your imagination. The problem comes when people are lazy and lift the story line and basic set-up intact, making only the most superficial of alterations.

To be completely safe, your new story must be so different from the other that not even its author would be able to spot the similarities.

Working smarter and more professionally

Of course, there's much more to etiquette than not indulging in theft and dirty tricks. There's a code of good practice to follow if you want to be taken seriously. Obeying these protocols and customs shows that you know what you're doing.

There are a variety of different conventions to observe, but here are a few handy dos and don'ts which we urge you to take on board. They will help to guide you through the manners minefield.

DO: give yourself plenty of time, so that you can ensure you submit your best work. Judges can tell when competition entries are obviously rushed, with writers throwing words on to the page in a frenzy at the very last minute. It may give those competitors an adrenalin buzz, but the end results are usually amateurish and quickly rejected in favour of slicker and more carefully prepared work.

Judges get annoyed with having to handle shoddy work. It is not only discourteous, but the unspoken message is that the writer didn't consider the competition important enough to warrant his time and concentration.

Time management is a vital skill for any writer. Plan your writing so that you give yourself time to finish the first draft comfortably before the closing date, and are then able to go through it a second time.

We'd suggest at least a two week safety margin. You'll be surprised what mistakes and potential improvements you'll spot when you view the work with fresh eyes. Those entries that snatch the top prizes may differ in many crucial ways, but they all have one thing in common – they are polished.

DO: get a friend, writing tutor or loved one to read through your work before you send it off. It's impossible to spot all your own mistakes and a second pair of eyes can save your blushes. It's notoriously difficult to spot mistakes on screen, so always check through hard copy print-outs or proofs.

DO: read the rules as soon as you receive them. You'd be surprised at the people who leave it to the last minute to enter and either don't bother to read the rules at all, or skim through them in a panic and fail to notice important restrictions. Failing to spot a vital rule is just as bad as deliberately ignoring it.

DO: keep a competitions log so that you can track the progress and success of your entries. It helps you to plan your writing schedule and lets you keep an eye on closing dates, when you should be revising/polishing an entry and when entries you've sent off to earlier comps are available to submit again.

A simple log will prevent you from getting into a muddle and submitting the same piece to two comps simultaneously or entering something that's already been a winner.

And, if you are a bit absent minded or scatty, it will save your blushes. Organisers often receive embarrassing notes from worried competitors saying things like: *If you've seen this before, I'm sorry* or *I can't remember whether this has been published or not.*

How you choose to draw up your log is up to you, but here's a simple example you might want to copy.

COMP DETAILS	ENTRIES SENT	CLOSING DATE	FEE	JUDGE (IF KNOWN)	RESULTS
Newland Writers Circle Comp	Poem: Life Is A Bowl of Cherries	12 Nov last yr	£3/$5	Jean Wright	3rd Place
Writers Bureau Annual Comp	Short Stories: Dead on Arrival Two Good to be True	2 Feb this yr	£7/$11	Iain Pattison	No Wins
Globelink Magazine Poetry Comp	Poem: Now You've Gone	31 May this yr	£4/$7	Jean Wright	Shortlisted

Using a grid like this helps you keep track of what you're sending out, what comps you've entered and how your entries fared. It also allows you to keep tabs on how much you are spending.

Recording the names of judges is particularly useful. In this example Jean Wright was judging both the Newland Writers Circle and Globelink comps. By having a log, our competitor knew not to submit *Life is a Bowl of Cherries* to the Globelink event as Jean would have already seen it in the earlier contest.

Of course, by noting that the poem had secured a third place he knew that it wouldn't be eligible for Globelink's comp when he read the rules prohibiting previous winners.

Look through your log regularly to check when it's safe to resubmit an unsuccessful entry. If you haven't heard anything after, say, four months from the closing date then you can assume that the piece hasn't won that tournament and you are free to try it elsewhere.

Keep the log as up to date as possible, perhaps inserting new information at the end of every week or fortnight.

This example is not, of course, the only way to draw up a log. Feel free to devise your own or to customise our example, adding any other columns you might think useful – like, for example, a column for the dates when you posted work.

Forbidden

Those are the things you should always do, but what should you avoid? Our suggested list of no-nos are:

DON'T: enter the same piece of work to the same competition two years running. The chances are it'll be the same judge as last time and even if he can't exactly place your work, he will recognise it – with a groan.

He will not be best pleased at having to go through the dubious delights of a repeat performance. He wants to believe that everything he reads will be new. It's just a waste of your money. If the adjudicator didn't like the piece twelve months ago, why should he suddenly value it now?

One thing guaranteed to send him into orbit is if he wrote a critique on your piece last year and you've submitted it again without changing a word!

DON'T: look upon a competition as a last chance dustbin for rejected articles, poems or short stories which are not good enough to be published, or which have failed to make the grade somewhere else. Contests attract the cream of the profession. They are all about excellence. The standard of writing in the average competition will be higher than most work found in a magazine slush pile – or even in its pages.

Be brutally honest with yourself. Don't waste your time and money if you know the piece isn't the best you can possibly achieve. You'd probably give yourself a better chance of success if you invested the entry fee money in a lottery ticket.

DON'T: send your only copy of a cherished piece of work. Most organisers don't keep entries after the final judging and will instruct the judge to destroy all manuscripts. So all your work will go up in smoke.

If organisers offer to return all entries accompanied by a stamped, self addressed envelope, make sure you enclose one and that it has the name of your story or poem on it, in case the envelope and your entry become accidentally separated.

Also make sure the envelope is big enough and postage is sufficient for the weight of the manuscript. Organisers won't subsidise you.

In some foreign competitions, organisers will request IRCs – international reply coupons – to a certain value for the return of manuscripts or to cover the cost of posting out an anthology of winners. You can get IRCs at main post offices.

DON'T: send in a rubber cheque to cover your entry – your work will be disqualified. Make sure there's enough cash in your account to cover the entries. If your cheque bounces, it will bounce you out of the competition.

Likewise, make sure you remember to actually attach the cheque to your entry form. Most organisers aren't going to bother chasing you up. They'll simply put your work on the eliminated pile.

And double check that you've sent the right amount of money for the number of entries you are submitting. A competition is difficult enough to run without the organisers having to worry about people who can't add up. If you send insufficient funds, some of your pieces will be taken out of the judging pile. Life being as cruel as it is, it's bound to be your best work.

If organisers ask you to send your entry fee in the form of stamps, make sure you send a number of small denomination stamps not one single large value stamp. They will want to use the stamps for admin – for sticking on letters – and will be looking for ordinary first and second class stamps. One mega stamp for a large sum will just give the organisers a headache – especially if they have to go to their local post office and plead for it to be exchanged.

DON'T: be tempted by offers of reduced entry fees for multiple submissions, no matter how attractive they may seem or how hard up you may be. It's likely that all the pieces you send will be lumped together in the judging pile so that the adjudicator will read them one after another.

If he hated your first effort, and sees the next piece is laid out in exactly the same manner, on the same type of paper, it will naturally colour his thinking towards it.

Alternatively, if the judge is starting to tire after a long reading session, you don't want all your work being viewed in the same jaundiced way.

We know it is slightly more expensive to send in entries individually but each piece of work will stand more chance if it is submitted on its own. For this reason, it's a good idea to wait a few days between submissions. This will help ensure your work is evenly spaced through the pile.

$$* \qquad * \qquad *$$

That sounds a lot to remember, doesn't it? But it's all just common sense really. This simple code of behaviour will ensure you'll always be seen as a serious contender.

One especially important thing to do is to enter as many competitions as you can. Not only will you increase your chances of success, but you'll help keep the competitions scene vibrant and healthy. And that's something we all want to see.

5

INSIDE THE MIND OF A JUDGE

Mention the word "judge" to most people and they immediately think of some stern-faced figure of authority dispensing justice from on high. Well, you will be glad to hear that competition judges aren't a bit like that. Not at all ... we're much worse!

Seriously, writers always seem a bit surprised when they meet us and find that – apart from the two heads and the awful sense of humour – we are much like everyone else. Often it's a bit of a let-down. We're expected to have magical powers or second sight, not just to be mere mortals with mortgages.

There are barrow-loads of misconceptions about judges, what they do, what powers they exercise and what motivates them. So in this chapter, we will try to correct a few wrong impressions. We'll take a good look at judges and ask: who are they; who appoints them and how do you please them?

Just who are judges?

Competition adjudicators are not – as you might think – evil, grinning sadists who enjoy rejecting people's work and poking holes in it. Neither are they people who walk round with their noses in the air, thinking themselves perfect or superior.

Mostly, they are ordinary, jobbing scribblers – short story writers, journalists and poets; people who love the world of writing and get as much of a buzz out of competitions as you do.

Usually they've been writing professionally for a number of years and will have had enough experience and success in their chosen genre to be able to speak knowledgeably about what works and what doesn't. And they'll probably be well known as magazine columnists or popular speakers on the writers' circle speaking circuit.

Most will undoubtedly have been competition junkies in the past, who've entered loads of comps and know exactly what it's like to send off work and then wait tensely to see if it has won. They'll have tasted failure like all competitors, and know how it hurts, but they'll also have had numerous competition wins to their credit.

But more importantly, they will have learnt the secrets of producing work that sizzles and stands out from the herd, and will recognise that same talent in the work of others.

In addition to being working writers, many judges are evening class teachers, workshop co-ordinators, writers' circle organisers, professional appraisers or script doctors, creative writing lecturers or distance learning tutors. They understand the writing game inside out.

Of course, some judges are household name writers – novelists and major league poets – whose involvement with a competition is guaranteed to give it maximum publicity and kudos. On occasion, a celebrity will be roped in to judge a major headline competition – especially one being run by a television programme, radio station or national newspaper or magazine.

Usually the actor, sports star, presenter or politician will be someone who has some experience of writing – even if it's only his autobiography!

Other judges are usually drawn from the ranks of editors. Most will run small press, literary or specialist magazines. They'll have the experience of wading through their slush piles to find good material and will have a trained eye for spotting work that will appeal to a large audience.

With single genre competitions – such as those for sci-fi, horror or children's stories – having specialist adjudicators can be a real boon for organisers, and ensures competitors are judged by someone with a sympathetic attitude.

What a judge looks for

This is an important thing to figure out. After all, if you can tell what an adjudicator itches to see then you can make sure your work fits the bill. Of course, judges differ in their likes and dislikes. Some favour gritty, realistic material, while others prefer more whimsical or sentimental writing.

There are also differences in their backgrounds, writing styles and the way they tackle the job. Poets may vary in approach to journalists or short story writers. Older writers may have a divergent outlook on life to younger authors, and there are subtle (or not so subtle!) differences between men and women.

But even allowing for these natural human variations, it's fair to say that there is a huge amount of common ground between all competition adjudicators.

No matter who they are – or what genre they're judging – they all look for work that is exceptional; pieces that make them sit up and pay attention, material that has something thrilling, new, provocative or challenging to say. Above all, they'll be looking for work that entertains and holds the reader enraptured.

Another way of thinking about it is that they are talent-spotting. They are searching for "star quality" writers who are:

- **Imaginative**. Someone whose power of imagination can amaze and inspire. Someone who can transport us to other worlds, or can make us see the familiar world in new – and intriguing – ways.

- **Original**. Everything about the work is innovative. It cries out that this is someone who is inventive, with something fresh to say.

- **Daring**. A competitor who fully understands the form and conventions of the genre, but breaks these for good effect – with confidence. Someone not afraid to experiment.

- **Blessed with flair and verve**. Someone with style and panache. A writer who embraces the freedom a comp offers to break away from formulae, the expected and the routine.

- **Able to write with emotional depth**. They produce material that has depth and passion, which can't fail to trigger feelings and responses from you.

- **In control of the material**. Skilled wordsmiths, those who can produce material that talks to the reader on different levels. People whose writing has sub-text, depth and nuance.

- **Professional in attitude**. They've turned in a neat, well presented script. It doesn't read as though it's rushed or thrown together.

- **Able to produce writing with the "Wow!" factor**. Competitors who can produce work that's knock-em-dead impressive – clever, attention-grabbing, has impact ... work that makes you say: *I wish I'd written that.*

- **Have the ability to present their work with a strong, individualistic voice**. Not only do they speak in a unique and powerful way, but they come across clearly and with personality, warmth and authority.

- **Humorous and keen observers of life**. Writing which can make readers smile, showing the amusing and absurd side of life. Writers who demonstrate a clear and profound understanding of human nature and what makes people tick.

Turn offs

A judge having to read anything up to a thousand entries is going to face the task with a certain amount of apprehension and weariness. It's only human nature. A pile of paper stacked four feet high is a daunting sight.

And it will be worse if he's judging several competitions in a row or two contests simultaneously. He may feel he has died and gone to adjudicator's hell.

He'll obviously aim to be as fair as possible, but he's not going to be reading everything with a happy grin and a song in his heart – especially when he's half way through the mountain of entries. So you owe it to yourself to make sure you stay on his right side, that you create a good impression.

If your entry contains anything that is irritating, nasty, amateurish, smug or simply gratuitous, it's likely to be a huge turn-off. And it only takes a moment to lose goodwill.

Make a point of finding out what things are likely to put off a judge. Always look through your work and ask yourself: *is there anything that is going to annoy him, or make him groan in despair.* If so, change it!

The following list isn't definitive but it does cover most of the major no-nos. We suggest you don't submit work that's:

- **Bitter or carping**. By all means use your writing to launch attacks on those you think are corrupt, dishonest, bigoted or dangerous. Speak out against injustice and evil. But beware seeming to be jaundiced in your attitude or unnecessarily nasty, offensive or smugly superior in tone.

- **Shoddily produced**. The inevitable message this conveys is that you thought the competition wasn't worth the effort. How a piece looks is as important as what it says. Scrappy work will be quickly discarded.

- **Difficult to decipher**. If the judge struggles to understand what you're saying – or trying to say – he won't have the time or inclination to code-break. That's why it's crucial to have a friend read through your work before submitting it, to spot anything ambiguous, cryptic or woolly.

- **Obviously done tongue in cheek**. No matter how hard you try to hide it, your lack of honesty and sincerity will show through. Never tackle a type of writing if you don't believe in its merits or cynically think it's so simplistic and easy that anyone can churn it out. Be especially careful with your motives when attempting a send-up. Remember that there's a thin line between producing an affectionate parody of a genre, and seeming to sneer at it.

- **Written in a stream-of-consciousness style that does not make sense**. If you want the strange and worrying workings of your subconscious scrutinised, go and see a psychiatrist. Don't inflict it on a competition judge – he's probably got enough psychological problems of his own!

- **Been created while under the influence of drink or drugs**. You may think what you penned in a state of chemically induced euphoria is profound and moving, but more than likely it'll just be gibberish. Beware of inner voices telling you that what you've written is a masterpiece – it'll be the booze talking.

- **Racist**. No competition will give bigots or extremists a platform to spread hate, intolerance and misery.

- **Sexist or ageist**. Apart from being a fairly unpleasant thing to do, how do you know who will read the piece in the course of the contest? The named judge might be a young man, but he may only be seeing a selection of the entries. The panel sifting through to compile an initial shortlist may be made up of women and pensioners. Some may even be women pensioners! Dare you risk upsetting them?

- **Seeking to poke fun at any minority**. Even if you don't mean any harm many readers will find this unacceptable and ill-considered. Beware scapegoating any group.

- **Seeking to ridicule the under-privileged, mentally disturbed or disabled**. If you're even tempted to do this, you should have a long hard look in the mirror.

- **Terminally depressing**. It's possible to write about any subject – even death – without plunging the reader into the depths of despair. Aim to be as optimistic and upbeat as the topic allows. Don't make the judge feel that there's only melancholy, sorrow and gloom in the world. With the pile of unread entries staring at him, he may just try to end it all.

- **Twee or cute**. No fluffy-tailed bunny rabbits, twinkling-eyed grannies, talking toasters, people too nice to be true, "gosh, super, jolly hockey sticks" dialogue, Enid Blyton villains who come quietly when the children unmask their dastardly deeds, or "It's a Wonderful Life" style guardian angels.

- **Designed to show how wonderful or knowledgeable the writer is**. No-one likes a show-off. You may be clever, talented, charming and fragrant, but leave it to others to sing your praises. Otherwise, people might think you're just big headed!

● **Didactic or preachy**. No-one likes listening to a lecture on morals or being told how to behave or what to think. If the judge needs to be preached to, he'll ring his mother!

● **Too religious**. Those who don't share your faith and zeal will find it makes them uncomfortable.

● **Pokes fun at religion**. Apart from the risk of ending up on an international hit list, there's no point in needlessly offending people. By all means make serious, valid, points – even critical ones – about faiths, but avoid seeing religion as an easy target for humour.

● **Party political**. Nothing is more guaranteed to start a punch-up than a "friendly" debate about politics. Be aware that your view of how the country should be run will differ dramatically from other people's – including, more than likely, the judge's. Keep your politics a secret between you and the ballotbox.

Breaking taboos

Perhaps the biggest turn-off is where the writer deliberately tries to shock or scandalise. This is something new writers often attempt, wrongly believing that the only way to make an impact is to alarm and startle the reader with gory descriptions, sickening imagery and excessive bad language.

Well, it may cause a stir and controversy in the cutting edge world of radical small-press magazines, where editors push the barriers of what is acceptable and what constitutes good taste, but in any normal competition it's guaranteed to ruin your chances.

It's vital to know where to draw the line, to be aware of what is permissible and what isn't. Shaking an audience out of its complacency is one thing, but there's no excuse for trying to "gross out" or mortify your readers.

63

In fact, we'd argue that there's no need for excessive use of sexual or violent imagery in any work, especially if it isn't central to the theme of the piece and is just there for titillation. Writing can still be extremely realistic – dark and disturbing, mean and moody – without resorting to cheap tactics.

We know that competitions offer more freedom of subject and style than most mainstream magazines, but there are still taboos that mustn't be broken.

Always avoid sexual swear words, any sex act that is illegal, any story or poem which glorifies violence, abuse or rape and any material that would obviously cross the good taste boundary – such as cannibalism, mutilation, bestiality, torture, incest and the humorous treatment of Aids.

It's basically a case of using common sense. You should instinctively know when you are heading on to dangerous territory. Don't risk your work being rejected for a tacky thrill.

Remember that the judge will be looking for a poem or short story that can safely be published in a mainstream magazine if it wins, and which won't offend an average, fair-minded audience. There's no room for pornography, erotica, sick humour or extreme violence.

Incidentally, even an erotica competition will insist that all sex is non-violent, legal and between consenting adults.

Can the judge guess the gender of a competitor?

People at writers' circles often ask this when either of us goes to talk to them. Our reply is: sometimes, sometimes not.

It's true that men and women often have a very different approach – a divergence of styles. Men tend to write about actions and their consequences, about tangible concrete things, while women tend to deal more with feelings and emotions; with concepts. But as with all generalities, there are many marked exceptions.

Often it's impossible to tell. Good writers can adopt a variety of styles and it wouldn't be the first time that a judge has picked a winner imagining the gritty plot-line to have been penned by a chunky mature male only to meet a diminutive teenage girl at the awards ceremony.

We know that we've both been fooled by pieces that have been weepy Kleenex specials yet turned out to be written by men. So you can never be 100 per cent sure of the gender of the entrant. And, as all entries are anonymous, the judge can only guess.

Will it influence him?

No – although it is a common misconception. We've frequently heard it said that a male judge will automatically pick a male winner. Men stick together. It's a world-wide "lads" conspiracy.

Apart from the fact that this view is laughably simplistic, it's also insulting. It doesn't say much about your faith in the judge's integrity or intelligence if you believe he would play favourites or have some sinister hidden agenda.

Even if the judge can tell the gender of a writer, or the writer's nationality or what part of the country he comes from, it won't influence his thinking. He'll judge a piece purely on its impact and entertainment value – **what** it says, not **who** is saying it ... or who he thinks is saying it! Of course, the same thing holds true for women judges. There's no secret sisterhood conspiracy. They don't look to pick women winners – just the most talented writers in the bundle of competitors.

It's worth pointing out here that judges usually can't tell a person's age either. This is a good thing, of course, unless the comp brief is to write an autobiographical piece.

Is it worth researching the judge?

Ah, now this is a more tricky question. There are opposing schools of thought on this one. There are those who say it's a useful way of getting to know what type of material will appeal to a particular adjudicator, and then there are those who say that it's impossible to "second-guess" a judge's likes or dislikes on any given day. It's a waste of time that would be better spent polishing and refining your entry.

Judges themselves can't agree – not even the authors of this book. Alison, as a poet, supports the "yes" camp, while Iain, as a short story writer, is against researching.

So it's probably better if you make up your own mind and act accordingly. Don't worry, we're not trying to squirm out of anything – we'll look at the subject in depth and explain the case both for and against so you can see which side convinces you.

The YES arguments:

Knowledge is power. The more you know about a judge the better. It's useful to learn a little about the judge's preferred style of writing, not to offer a pale pastiche but to catch on to the right wavelength. For example, if a judge has expressed a dislike of stories told in the first person, or of unrhymed poetry, it would be daft to send such an entry.

Judges often write articles for writing magazines. They also produce detailed comments after every competition, which are often published as well as being sent to competitors. So it shouldn't be too difficult to find out what turns him on – or, more importantly, turns him off.

It can save you a lot of grief. If a judge hates children you know that your child appreciation piece will fall on deaf ears.

So, it may be a good idea to keep a dossier of judges. The competitions world is small and close knit, and the same names crop up time after time as adjudicators – especially as writing groups running contests often recommend judges to each other. You'll soon spot the regulars.

In this dossier you can file anything you learn about them. Keep notes on any points that arise within their reports on other competitions, whether you've entered them or not. For example: Alison has a particular dislike of metrical poetry that strays from its particular metre, and she has said so frequently in her magazine columns.

Because they've read this and taken note of it, people have said to her: *I never enter a comp when you're judging because I can't cope with metre.*

There are plenty of other poetry judges who don't share this hang-up – it's not universal by any means – so a little bit of research has enabled competitors to avoid sending their work to a comp where it was doomed to failure.

The NO arguments:

It's not worth spending time researching the judge as he'll pick the best of the bunch – not the story that most resembles his own style. He may be impressed by work that is the direct opposite of the type of writing he'd normally produce. In other words, by someone tackling a subject the judge wouldn't dream of touching.

He won't be looking for a clone of himself. His own work may offer few – perhaps no – clues.

In addition, he may have been given instructions by the organisers on the type of story/poem they want – or don't want – to win. He may have been asked to specifically pick a winner that's upbeat/emotional/topical/humorous etc and you won't be privy to this inside information. So your investigations may point you in the wrong direction.

And what if the judge is operating outside of his normal field – an adult writer being asked to judge children's stories, for example? What good will studying him or his writing do then?

Besides, the "advertised" judge may not actually see every entry. He may only be picking a winner from a shortlist that's been selected by the organisers – none of whom will be announced or named. Unless you know how everyone involved thinks, any research on the judge is an academic exercise.

Another point worth considering is that it's also not unknown for a judge to drop out just before the closing date of a competition because of ill health, or a disagreement with the organisers, and for a replacement to be hastily appointed. If there isn't time to publicise the substitution, you won't know. You'll have a profile on the wrong person.

It's better to spend your time making sure your own work is as slick and polished as you can make it. Any research you do should be looking at the previous winners in any given competition and getting a feel for what makes a prize-grabbing entry.

Always keep a copy of any anthology of top competition stories/poems and any magazine that publishes winners. If a successful entry is displayed on a website, print if off and keep it.

Where we all agree

Now, we don't want you to get the idea that the competitions world is bitterly torn apart and divided over this. It's all just a question of personal preference, of different emphasis. Don't worry too much about it. Do whatever makes you happy.

You'll be pleased to hear that there is one point where we all agree and that's where the same judge adjudicates the same competition year after year.

If you routinely enter it each time then it's worth looking at what makes the judge tick and looking to see if you can spot trends in what he selects as winners. But be sensible – the really important thing has always got to be the standard of your own work.

6

HOW A COMPETITION IS ORGANISED

By now you might be thinking that actually organising your own competition would be a lot of fun – and lucrative. You'd be right. It is hard work, but it's very rewarding, and although you can come a cropper, you should be able to make some cash for your writers' club from a competition, and you will certainly put your group on the map.

Just think of the benefits you could derive. We've already mentioned fundraising, but you could add that it brings kudos to your writing group, and lets the world know that you're out there and doing something. It gives you the chance to promote a specific branch of writing, and help writers by offering them an outlet for their work. You are extending their interest in the craft of writing, and this resurgence of interest has the knock-on effect of helping small press magazines and other publishers whose sales are increased. You are giving work to local printers or copy shops and to your selected judge.

Give yourself a hearty pat on the back and then reach for the calculator.

First do the sums

Before you start to think about the literary side of running a writing competition, you need to think about money. Unless you're a millionaire philanthropist with a desire to patronise the arts (and if you are, please send us your name and address) you will want to end up on the right side of the balance sheet. Careful planning is the only way to achieve this – and even then, it isn't guaranteed.

Think realistically about all the expenses involved. You will need to advertise your competition, fork out for postage and stationery, print entry forms, pay a judge, budget for prizes, and possibly arrange an awards ceremony and/or publish an anthology of winning entries. All of these things cost money, and probably more money than you expected.

You will probably have to compromise somewhere along the line. Entry forms do not have to be hand printed on vellum, nor does the awards ceremony have to take place at the top hotel in town. You can settle for neat forms and a pleasant venue without breaking the bank.

You may think in grand terms about offering the richest prize in the literary world for your competition, but that might mean charging a ridiculously high entry fee to ensure enough returns to cover the prize. It would be a better idea to make the prize more modest and the entry fee more affordable.

While you are thinking about how much to offer in prize money, consider the possibility of having a special prize that will catch the writer's eye. Attendance at a writing course or the gift of a word processor would be marvellous; but the promise of a good reference book, a year's subscription to a small press magazine, a clutch of novels or poetry books, or even a supply of good quality stationery would be a draw.

The promise to publish winning entries in anthology form or perhaps on the Internet is attractive. If an editor or agent is willing to look at the top entries, many writers will be tempted to compete.

You may be able to underwrite your prizes by obtaining sponsorship. If individuals or companies can be persuaded to help out with cash or gifts, one of your headaches vanishes immediately. Remember the saying, though, that there's no such thing as a free lunch.

For example, if a local bookshop offered copies of a writing handbook for the five best entries, you might be expected to print their advertisement on the entry forms. You may have no qualms about doing this, and feel that the relationship is symbiotic. If, however, a local worthy offered you a cash sum for a first prize on the condition that he should assist with the judging, it might be better to decline politely. Alison was once asked to do the final adjudication of a competition from a shortlist compiled by a sponsor. The thirty poems she was shown were sweet and sentimental, but none of them would have passed the hurdle of the initial scan if she had been involved from the start of the process.

Before you make your final decision about prizes, have a look at what other competitions are offering. This will give you a rough idea of how many noughts should appear on the winner's cheque and some guidelines about the going rate to charge for entry fees.

Remember that you can ask for a considerably higher fee per entry if you offer a critique on each piece submitted. The judge is taking on a huge workload if you do this, though, so be aware that most of the extra money will be directed to him. You could, perhaps, agree a sum for each critique with the adjudicator and then top it up with a small extra sum for your coffers; but as this service adds so much to the cost for each entry, don't be too greedy about the extent of your rake-off or the fee required will deter a lot of competitors.

However you decide to set the financial level of your comp, you will need to get enough entries to cover costs. That means advertising so that the likely competitors know you are there; so that's where we shall begin.

Advertising

As soon as you have decided to run a competition, start advertising it. Don't worry if the closing date is several months away. Writers can be amazingly methodical about filing comp information (after all, they have read Chapter Four) and will keep a note of your comp no matter how far in advance they hear about it.

Television advertisements cost an arm, a leg and a couple of kidneys. Your local radio station will not have as large an audience as primetime TV, but if you approach them with the information that a local group is running a writing competition, they will often invite you onto a magazine programme to talk about it.

Before you go into the studio, check that you have all the relevant information at your fingertips. You will need to know the identity of the judge and the precise requirements of the competition – the maximum number of words for a short story, the theme about which people should write, the maximum number of lines for a poem etc. You must know what prizes are on offer, and whether an anthology of winners will be produced. You need to sell the idea of the comp during the few minutes you'll have on air.

During the interview you will have the chance to invite listeners to write in for details. Make sure you ask them to send a stamped, self addressed envelope so that you save on stationery and postage costs. If you ask them to phone for a form, remember that you'll have to provide the stationery and postage. Alternatively, if you have the facilities you could provide an e-mail address they could contact or a website where they could download details.

You will not be paid for making your broadcast, but nor will you have to pay anything for the airtime. Make sure you leave all the details in writing at the reception desk and a pile of entry forms in the studio foyer.

If you can get a slot with the radio station at an early stage in the competition, you might be able to appear and give an update on how the comp is going nearer to the closing date. This extra plug should bring you another cluster of entries.

Advertising in writing magazines does cost, but you should be able to get your competition mentioned in the editorial pages or comps list for no charge. If you are hoping for an editorial feature about your comp, don't simply send in an entry form to a magazine – send a press release, putting all the essential information in the form of a brief article. You can press home the point that it is not intended as a paid advert by typing PRESS RELEASE across the top. Your material will probably be edited and some of the information omitted. So make sure you give the address to which people can apply for entry forms near the beginning. Again be sure to ask for a sae.

If, however, the magazine has a designated page listing forthcoming competitions, then sending a copy of your entry form is enough.

Out of interest, you can even track which outlets yield the greatest response in terms of people requesting entry forms and then actually entering the competition by feeding a check initial into your name and address. For example, people might have to apply to John F. Smith if they saw the information about the comp in *Freelance Market News*, or to John O. Smith if it was mentioned in *Orbis* magazine.

Your main aim in advertising is to place entry forms in the hands of people who are likely to use them. You can blitz a town with them, leaving them in the tourist information centre, local hotels and shops, even at hairdressers, and in doctors' and dentists' waiting rooms. But you will not get very much response. So how do you make sure you are not spending a fortune on photocopying entry forms that will become scrap paper for non-writers to scribble shopping lists on?

You can blitz the right bits of town. The reference library, arts centre or further education college are places many writers pass through. A pile of entry forms left there will at least be seen by the people you want to see them. Send your poetry forms to a specialised poetry library, and you should get an even better return.

You can enlist all the members of your writers' group to enclose an entry form each time they correspond with a writer friend. Persuade them to send forms with their Christmas cards. (Yes, there are writers who will immediately stop panic buying and present wrapping in order to pen a short story.) Urge them to take a bundle of forms to any writing seminar, course or lecture they attend. Most organisers are happy for such information to be distributed on these occasions.

Some small press publications will send out your entry forms with every copy of their magazine. You will probably be charged for this service, but it may be cost effective. The sums won't be enormous, and you will know that your forms are going directly to the people who want them. Contact a few editors, and check how many copies of the magazine they distribute and what they would charge for the service.

We have mentioned the *Small Press Guide* published by Writers' Bookshop previously. Many of their entries indicate whether the magazine in question will accept advertising or inserts and how much this will cost.

You can even get together with the organiser of another writing competition closing within a few weeks of yours. If each of you agrees to include the other's entry form along with your own when anyone applies, you will double the number of forms arriving in the hands of prospective entrants. Don't worry about this apparent consorting with the opposition – the people who enter comps are looking out for all the opportunities they can find, and will probably enter both comps rather than choosing between the two.

In fact, there are more reasons why it can be useful to get together with the organisers of other competitions. Writers are renowned for being generous souls, and you can get all sorts of help and insider tips from organisers. These will help you to operate efficiently, and avoid the inevitable problems that crop up. You will also have a shoulder to cry on, someone to commiserate with, someone to celebrate with, and the chance to discuss the merits and shortcomings of various judges.

Help!

Organising a competition does involve work, and becomes a lot easier if you can get a team of people to help you. If you are asked to be the organiser, look for a couple of volunteers who will constitute a subcommittee. Don't accept too many, or you'll never get anything done. Three people is an ideal number.

Begin by making a list of all the things you will have to do. You might end up with something like this:

● Draw up the entry form, conditions and list of rules
● Organise prizes
● Decide whether you will be publishing an anthology
● Plan the distribution of awards
● Decide on a judge
● Liaise with the judge
● Word process the entry forms
● Photocopy them
● Distribute entry forms
● Submit press releases
● Receive and process entries and list fees received
● Bank the fees
● Send entries to the judge
● If relevant, make arrangements for an awards ceremony
● Confirm the identity of the winners
● Notify winners
● Prepare prizes for distribution
● If relevant, collate material for inclusion in anthology
● Arrange printing and distribution of anthology
● Collate results and/or judge's report and photocopy them for distribution

- Prepare press releases announcing the results and, if applicable, details of next year's competition
- Send press releases to everyone who helped with initial publicity
- If relevant, prepare entry forms for next year's competition.

When you have worked your way through your checklist and decided what is to be done, the work can be packaged into three chunks and divided among the committee. It makes sense to keep some aspects of it together. For example, it is useful if the person receiving the entries can also deal with the banking; there is continuity if one person deals with all the advertising, liaison etc. For the most part, simply decide on the areas each member of the comp committee would like to control – but make sure that everything is co-ordinated through one individual. You've heard the one about too many cooks ...

Assuming that you've already assimilated the ideas about finance and advertising mentioned at the beginning of this chapter, let's have a look in more detail at the other steps you should follow.

Before the comp is launched

Right at the beginning of the process, you will need to draw up an entry form with rules and conditions. The easiest way to do this is by looking back at Chapter Three and selecting those conditions which seem most useful for your purposes, and then getting hold of all the other competition entry forms you can find to see how everyone else approaches the task.

Decide whether to set a theme for the competition or to leave it open, remembering that open comps always attract more entries, whereas themed comps tend to attract more original work. Similarly you will need to work out whether you require a particular style or form of writing, eg specify whether you want to read a first person story in a short story comp, or a sonnet in a poetry comp.

State the maximum length for entries, which should be confirmed with the judge in advance. Prose manuscripts are measured in words and poetry in lines. If you are running a competition for a piece of drama, it is appropriate to specify a number of minutes' playing time. The longer the entries you accept, the more you must be willing to pay the judge who has to read them all.

Establish where you stand on the question of previously published/broadcast material. Define your rule as clearly as you can to avoid any loopholes.

Fix the competition's closing date. Remember, you need to accommodate the judge's schedule – there is no point in closing a competition the day before he jets off for a month's holiday. You should also avoid having the same closing date as a much bigger writing competition. Your contest will not be able to compete with it in terms of advertising and prizes. Your entries will be depleted – not so much because of the glittering prizes the other comp is offering, but because their entry fees are likely to be on the high side, and writers need to balance the books like everyone else.

There's no problem with closing at the same time as a smaller competition, on a similar scale to yours. As we said earlier, entrants are likely to attempt both.

Decide how you intend to keep the identity of entrants secret during the judging process. This is important as you will want the judge not only to be impartial, but to be seen to be impartial.

The easiest thing is to advise competitors not to put any identifying marks on the manuscript. Instead, get them to put their name and address on a separate sheet, or on the entry form which should also contain the name of their story.

Put an entry number on the manuscript, and the same number on the sheet/form. Keep these sheets separate. Don't let the judge see them. We'll talk about what to do with these later in the chapter.

State clearly how much people will have to pay to enter, and what the prizes will be. This is where you have to take a gamble. You need to charge a realistic fee, one that will cover costs but will not deter people from entering. Check out all the other comps that are running at the same time as yours, and try to keep your fees on a similar level to theirs. As a very rough guide, the entry fee should be about half a percent of the total prize fund. (Prizes can be smaller or entry fees higher if you are running the competition to raise funds for charity.) Don't forget to add as options the cost of a personal critique and/or a copy of the winners' anthology, if you want to go down this road.

Talking of this, if you are planning to produce an anthology of winning pieces, start on some of the groundwork. Decide how simple or elaborate you wish the book to be, and get some quotations from printers. As long as you can show them the quality of publication you require, and tell them roughly how many pages there will be, you should be able to compare rates on an equal basis and choose your firm accordingly. Do check a few companies. Prices vary enormously, and paying too much for the anthology is a quick way of eating up your profits.

When you are budgeting for the anthology, you will need to take into consideration whether you will give free copies for those people whose work is included or charge winners. In addition, you may need a courtesy copy for the judge, a couple of copies for your group's archives and, if desired, review copies. So don't just look at the unit price and add a small amount of money for postage.

Remember that eye-catching prizes draw entries as well as eyes. As we outlined earlier, a gift can be a pleasing incentive.

It's not a good idea to be vague about prizes. Some comps state that the prize fund will consist of a proportion – say 70% – of the total entry fees. If only two people enter, this is not a great incentive.

Check with the members of your group how much of a loss they feel they could support. If you intend to run competitions on a regular basis, start small, with modest prizes and entry fees. If you are fortunate enough to build up a balance, you can be more ambitious next year. If not, cutting your losses should not be ruinous.

You should specify on the entry form who will be judging the competition, but say that he could be changed at the organisers' discretion in the case of problems. If the judge is only going to make a final adjudication from entries that have been pre-selected, this too should be stated. We'll look at this in more detail a little further on.

It's a good idea to request a sae from everyone, so that you can contact the writers after the competition. This means that they all have the opportunity to receive the list of winners and a judge's report; that you can circulate information about any future competitions and that you don't even have to pay postage to notify the winners. Also, if people send in a sae you have a double check of their address, which some of them will omit from the entry form or sheet of titles.

Three other points you may wish to add to the entry form are:

● No entries will be returned, so it is vital to keep a copy
● The judge's decision is final, and no correspondence will be entered into
● Those wishing to have notification that their entries have arrived safely must enclose a stamped addressed postcard for that purpose.

Believe us, you will save yourself no end of trouble and hassle if you make these stipulations on the entry form. If, however, you really want to return copies of the work, make sure you request a sae from each competitor. There is no need to burden yourself with extra costs and trouble. If a manuscript arrives without a sae hold on to it for three months after the adjudication. Unless the writer has requested it within that time, you can throw it out without any compunction. And don't compromise on the second point. No judge will want to get into a dialogue with a competitor, and it is better to make this clear from the outset.

If you want to publish a winners' anthology you should mention it on the form but don't definitely promise to bring out the volume unless you are completely convinced that you will sell enough to break even or that you can afford to make a loss on the deal.

Get entrants to tick a box on the entry form saying whether they would be interested in buying an anthology. If they do, you will have a good idea of how many copies to print, but exercise caution. People may change their minds or be put off if they don't turn out to be a winner.

Even if you have a good idea of numbers, you will still need to make some extra copies for contingencies. Don't worry if you find you have printed too many. You can always suggest to the entrants in your next competition that buying a copy of the previous anthology will give them some idea of the quality of work that has been commended in the past.

Producing an anthology is an attractive way of celebrating your competition. It brings added kudos to your writers' group, and collects together in one volume all the excellent work that would otherwise have been dissipated through a multitude of small press magazines. Some writers are thrilled to appear in a winners' anthology, whether they actually won prizes or only made it to the shortlist. On the downside, the publication of an anthology will bring with it a huge workload and additional expense.

If you do decide to go for the anthology, check that the judge is willing to select the requisite number of pieces to go into it. This is seldom a problem, as it simply involves choosing the best near misses from the shortlist. Also check that he will write a foreword or brief comment to be included – again, this isn't asking too much if he is going to submit a competition report anyway.

Selecting a judge

We said that you should announce on the entry form who is to judge the competition, and this is one of the most important decisions you will have to make. Writers feel most confident about entering a competition that is judged by another writer. This might sound like stating the blindingly obvious, but it's surprising just how many writers' groups decide to appoint a celebrity from a different sphere simply because of a personal contact. A politician, sports personality or TV star may have a name people recognise, but does not necessarily know a lot about writing.

There is, of course, a reason for this. The advantage of employing a celebrity as judge is that you can attract a lot of good free publicity for your competition on the basis of the big name, and many successful personalities will be prepared to judge without charging a fee. But if you are tempted to try someone from this category, be prepared for a knock-back. They may well be inundated with such requests.

Within the field of writing, always make sure you approach somebody whose expertise lies in the right genre. The editor of your local paper or one of his staff would be ideal to judge a competition for a journalistic feature, but might not be the right person to select a winning poem. If the competition is for the opening of a novel then an agent or representative of a publishing house could be a good judge.

Involving a small press editor or a mainstream magazine editor can have beneficial spin-offs for competitors. Alison was present at the prizegiving of a short story comp judged by the fiction editor of a women's magazine. He commissioned the top three stories on the spot, and encouraged several of the other entrants to send their work to the magazine for his attention.

With this in mind, you could always ask a prospective judge who runs a publication whether he would be willing to consider printing winning entries, and if so mention the fact on the entry forms. It could attract a lot more entries.

Where to look

Most competitions are adjudicated by writers. If you don't know any writers personally who might be suitable as a judge, it's quite easy to get some introductions. Your local arts board or reference library will have lists of writers in your area, and they often keep lists, too, of those writers who are willing to give talks. If you are planning to hold an awards presentation where the adjudicator is asked to speak, it might be useful to consider this.

Writing magazines will often put you in touch with writers whose work you have seen in their pages. Don't expect them to give out addresses, but they are usually willing to forward a letter to one of their contributors on your behalf. (Remember to stamp the letter and put the name of the addressee on the envelope and also supply a sae inside for the writer to respond to you.) Authors of books on creative writing are often willing to judge your competition, and they can be contacted via the publisher.

If you are trying to contact a poet, *The Poetry Society* at 22 Betterton Street, London WC2H 9BU is particularly helpful in this respect.

The Writers Bureau and Freelance Market News are also happy to suggest writers who are experienced judges.

If you contact other groups who have run competitions, they will be able to tell you who to ask and who to avoid. Creative writing tutors at your local college should also have plenty of contacts. Or simply cast a net among any writers you know to see whether they can make recommendations. Writing is a small world, and authors tend to network like mad. You will soon have a growing list of potential judges on your hands.

Don't worry if you can't find a judge on your own doorstep. With electronic mail and efficient parcel delivery, it is easy to keep in touch with a judge who lives at the opposite end of the country. The one slight problem could arise if you intend to bring him to your area for the prizegiving. You might find that his travelling expenses come to more than his fees, and a lot more than you bargained for when you did the sums in the first place.

Agree what he'll do

Talking of which, you must agree with the judge exactly what payment will be made and what is expected of him right at the beginning. There are two basic methods. You can either agree a global set fee to cover the adjudication, selection of anthology contents (if applicable), the provision of a report to be sent to competitors and, if you are having an award ceremony, making a short speech on that occasion and presenting the prizes. In poetry comps, the judge is often asked to read a selection of his poems to round off the evening and this, too, should be taken into account.

The other method is to agree a "per entry" payment, where the judge receives a set fee for each story, article or poem considered. This usually includes the provision of the report, but you must be prepared to pay an additional fee if you require a more lengthy article assessing the submissions. You will have to pay, too, for the judge to attend the prize-giving.

If you haven't a clue how much to offer for this service, ask around and find out how much people are paid as an hourly rate for teaching at night-school in your area. Double the rate for each hour the judge will be "on show" distributing prizes, giving a speech or reading from his own work. Then halve the rate for each hour the judge will be travelling to and from the venue. Add on reasonable travelling expenses, remembering that it costs more than the price of the petrol for a judge to come by car. If public transport is used, you may need to cover the cost of a taxi from the station.

In either case, don't forget that you will have to agree a higher fee for those entrants who require a critique of their work.

If you choose the second method of payment, you can economise by making a preliminary selection from the entries, weeding out the absolute no-hopers. If you can pare your entry by 30%, you cut your expenses. But you must agree this policy with the judge from the outset. Not all adjudicators are willing to work in this fashion, and you may find you have to show the judge every entry or find another judge.

Most judges prefer to be given sole responsibility for the adjudication, although many are willing to compromise about the initial selection. Some organisers feel, however, that two heads are better than one and prefer to appoint two or even three judges. Again, this must be agreed from the outset, and the combination of judges must be happy to work together. Those who have had a bad experience of collaborating will run a mile rather than agree to this situation, so you must make quite certain that everyone understands the ground rules before you print entry forms bearing the judges' names.

Up and running

When all the rules have been decided upon and the judge is appointed, print and start circulating your entry forms. You can print extra forms at any time, of course, but you are likely to need a lot more than you first think. If you have arranged to send forms to the Poetry Library, for instance, and for circulation in a small press magazine, you will need a thousand or more before you even start to send forms out to people who make individual enquiries.

Be prepared to send the forms out months in advance of the competition, and be ready to accept the entries as soon as they start to roll in. Some people are incredibly efficient, and will submit material six months or more before the closing date. Never turn an entry away, requesting that it should be re-submitted at a later date! The chances are the competitor might lose interest in the competition – and if you have had the opportunity to bank a fee a long time before the closing date, you could be earning interest on that fee for quite some time.

Send out your press releases to small press and writing magazines and to your local radio station at least nine months ahead of the closing date. Many small press magazines are published only three or four times a year, so require a copy in good time for it to be of use to their readers.

Given that you need to leave the readers a few weeks to assimilate all the contents of the magazine, you may find that requests for entry forms arrive months after the information was printed. It's frustrating to realise you have missed out on a score of competitors just because you didn't allow enough lead time between submitting the information to the magazine and the closing date of your comp.

If you are setting a specific theme rather than allowing writers to delve into their "freezer" of material and submit something for an open comp, you should give people at least three months to prepare their work. Don't expect too much response from anyone requesting an entry form within six weeks of the competition. Writers are usually busy people, and simply may not find time to write something new that reaches an appropriate standard.

This is not the case, of course, with an open competition, for which entry forms requested within a week of the closing date can bring in submissions. You might receive nothing except "bottom drawer" material – but if it prompts the writer to focus on his writing skills and comes with an entry fee, everyone still benefits.

As each entry comes in, it will need to be processed. Check that it has the requisite fee and that the writer's identity is submitted in the correct way. If these points have not been observed, or if the entry breaks other competition rules by exceeding the word limit, for example, disqualify it. You can be ruthless about this. You will soon get tied up in red tape and files of pending entries if you're not.

Having established the rules of your competition, it is up to you to decide how rigorously they should be enforced. As we said, some rules need to be observed strictly, such as the length limitation, anonymity of the author and publication status. Others, however, are a matter of convenience rather than necessity, such as the requirement for work to be double spaced, or presented on A4 paper. Some organisers will only process entries arriving before the closing date. Others will accept work postmarked by the closing date. As long as you follow the same policy in all cases, you can use a little common sense in your handling of the entries.

Some organisers contact competitors, offering them the chance to correct problems. Others do not bank the cheque of a competitor who submits an incorrect entry. You are not morally obliged to do either of these things – most organisers don't!

As soon as you receive the entry, number it and put the same number on the identifying paper, whether it's the actual entry form or a separate sheet. If you give a new number to each piece of writing entered, you will always know exactly how many pieces have been submitted, which helps when you come to balance the books.

Alternatively, you may prefer to give each competitor a number, and put that same number on every piece if he has sent in multiple entries. Although you will not be able to check on the number of entries at a glance if you do this, you will be giving the judge some information regarding the multiple entries. This may prove valuable if you have stipulated that no individual may win more than one prize.

But conversely, you may like to split multiple entries from one competitor so that the judge is not confronted with the same voice speaking from ten consecutive manuscripts. Shuffle the papers about a bit. It doesn't matter if the judge does not receive them in numerical order. He will probably be able to identify multiples by the same paper and typeface, and if he hated the first manuscript he encountered, he will approach the rest of that writer's entries with less than enthusiasm. But he may be able to look at the multiple entries with a fresh and fairer eye if he reads other work in between.

Establish two files, one for the numbered manuscripts, the other for the numbered identifying papers. Make sure you never put anything into one without the equivalent sheet going into the other. Double check everything. You can guarantee that if one poem or story in a thousand cannot be linked with its author, that will be the winner.

Some organisers make an additional check by keeping a competition ledger, either in a notebook or on computer. (It goes without saying that computer records should always be backed up.) The ledger consists of a list of names, addresses and telephone numbers copied from the identifying paper, the number of manuscripts entered and their titles, and the fee received. The ledger becomes a permanent record in the case of queries raised months after the competition when the files of papers have been discarded. It also provides you with a mailing list for future competitions or events.

Bank the fees on a regular basis. If a cheque bounces, disqualify the entry the moment you get the bad news from the bank. There are always a few rubber cheques, and it would be iniquitous if the first prize went to a competitor who had not contributed an entry fee.

Incidentally, it's a good idea to talk to the staff at the bank in advance of the comp to let them know that you'll be paying in a large number of very small cheques. Some banks are unhappy about this, and demonstrate their unhappiness by stinging you with excessive bank charges. If your competition is running on a shoestring budget, this can wipe out any profit and even leave you in debt. If the bank makes a charge for multiple small cheque clearance, change your bank. Some are far more reasonable than others – you just have to shop around a little.

Before the close of the competition, it is a sensible idea to confirm arrangements for any prize-giving ceremony. Before we talk about the arrangements it's worth spending a few moments looking at the pros and cons of organising a prize winners' event. Not all competition organisers bother. Some merely send out prize cheques through the post.

The advantages of a special evening are that it gives you a chance to meet the winners face to face. This means you'll get an opportunity to see how delighted the successful writers are and it will help make all the hard work you've put in seem worthwhile. It will also give you a chance to meet the judge.

A high profile event helps give your contest that sheen of prestige and offers your group extra visibility in the writing world. You can boost this coverage by inviting a photographer from the local paper to take pictures of the happy winners, standing beside the judge.

Of course, holding a ceremony is not always possible or desirable. If the comp attracted a small number of entries then any extra expenditure might eat up the modest profit you made. Then there may be problems if the winners are from the other side of the country and would have difficulty getting there.

You'll have to pay the judge extra to attend and make a speech and if you've had a less than smooth relationship with the judge, meeting him in person might be the last thing you want.

It's up to you to decide. An event isn't compulsory but it can be a nice way to round off the venture.

If you do decide to host an evening you will need to organise premises large enough to entertain the number of guests you envisage, and might even wish to lay on some refreshments. This may be no more than a cup of tea and a biscuit, or it may be a cheese and wine reception, or even a more formal supper.

Double check the timing of the booking. You need to find out at what time your venue is available, and whether it is open or you will have to obtain a key. Make sure you know when you have to vacate the premises, too.

Alison once attended an awards ceremony in a town hall. It was due to be followed by a poetry reading by the judge. In the event, people chatted for a bit too long over a glass of wine and snacks between the prizegiving and the reading. The caretaker subsequently bundled everyone out of the building half way through the reading, declaring that he didn't get paid overtime and had no intention of staying any longer.

Keep receipts for any payments you make in connection with the awards ceremony. You will need them when you come to claim your expenses and balance the books.

After the closing date

It is tempting to sit back with a sigh when you reach the closing date. After all, you have had a frantically busy month. Most of your entries will have arrived during the past three or four weeks, and every post should have brought you another flood of manuscripts. And the good news is – yes, you get a couple of weeks off.

It's a good idea to wait until a few days after the closing date if you have not specified on the entry form that pieces must be RECEIVED by that date. Then bundle the package of numbered manuscripts off to the judge with an entry form (to remind him of the rules). Make sure that they are parcelled securely, and send them by a reliable delivery firm.

Unless you have express permission to do so, don't send work by any means that requires a signature on receipt. Most judges have a job, and there is nothing more irritating than having to make a thirty mile round trip after work to collect a parcel which has to be signed for.

Make sure you allow the judge plenty of time to come to a decision. Not everyone reads swiftly. It is not always possible to drop everything else in your life to concentrate on comp entries; and remember, a judge may have other commitments. Some judges like to leave a period of a few days or a couple of weeks between an initial trawl of the entries and a more studied reading. As a general rule, allow a week per hundred entries submitted, and a week in hand.

This should allow time for the adjudication to be completed and the report to be written. If critiques are required, allow an extra week for each fifty entries on which comment is needed. This is particularly important. Iain once ended up on his knees after agreeing to critique every entry in a short story comp, and having only two weeks to complete the lot.

When the judge has reached a decision, he will contact you with the numbers and titles of the winning entries. All you have to do is to marry the numbers and titles with the names and addresses in your folder, and you will have identified the winners. That is the best part. You will have the pleasure of writing notes of congratulation, enclosing winners' cheques or inviting the authors to the awards ceremony.

As soon as you have done that, it's important to notify the other entrants who sent a sae of the results of the competition, and to send them the judge's report. If you have already decided to repeat the process next year, make sure you can send out the new entry form with the results. This may seem premature, but it is surprising how many competitors are delighted to have so much notice of a competition, and will submit their entries promptly. Also, it saves on postage – you don't have to write to them later at your own expense.

When you have let the competitors know the results, don't forget to contact all the magazine editors and radio presenters who were kind enough to provide you with free advertising. You should let them know the results as a matter of courtesy but doing so serves another useful purpose. It underlines the fact that the competition really did take place, that some writers were awarded prizes, and that yours was a bona fide enterprise.

By extending this courtesy you are not only completing a moral obligation to inform the media of the results – you are also maintaining a good relationship which will be valuable the next time you are running a competition.

And afterwards ...

When the prizegiving ceremony is over and the winners' anthology has been launched to critical acclaim, award yourself a hefty pat on the back for all the work you have accomplished. Then check the figures. If you have made a considerable profit, congratulate yourself, and your team, on their achievement. If you have made a modest profit or just broken even, don't start to agonise over all the hours of work for a tiny return. Again, be pleased that you are on the right side of the balance sheet.

If, however, you have made a loss on the competition, don't get depressed. Instead, think back to the reasons you held the comp in the first place. You have put your writers' group on the map. You have been able to reward the writing efforts of the winners, and may even have set them on the route to greater successes. You have retained the services of an adjudicator, giving him employment. In turn, his comments on the report will help any writer who reads carefully to learn more about his craft. So award yourself a gold star or a large gin, and bask in the satisfaction of a job well done.

Better luck next time

Don't give up. Go through your records and analyse why the competition didn't make a profit. It's possible that only one key element was wrong – perhaps you gave away too much in prizes or paid too much for printing the entry forms. See if you can tweak the arrangements for your next attempt, learning from your experiences this time.

What? You're never going to run a competition ever again? It was too exhausting. That's what everyone says immediately afterwards. Give it a few weeks for your batteries to recharge, and you'll be thinking differently. So it may have been chaos, a logistical nightmare, but hey it was fun too. And there wasn't a dull moment.

Perhaps it wasn't so bad after all. Maybe it would be okay to have another go. In fact, it might be worth starting to plan it right this moment. Now, where's next year's diary ...

THE WORLD OF
SHORT STORY COMPETITIONS

Well, I think we've talked enough for the moment about the generalities of competitions – how they are run, how judges think, what they look for in entries and the most effective way of tackling any contest.

Now it's time to look at each of the main specialist areas in some depth. In the next three sections we will examine how to excel in short stories, poetry and article writing.

In the following chapter Alison will take a comprehensive look at the world of poetry comps and how to do well in them. In Chapter Nine I'll do the same for articles. But just now, I'm going to talk about short story competitions, and in particular why so many writers fail to win. It's very much a personal view (that's why I use the first person throughout) but you will find that many judges share my thoughts and prejudices.

And, although this chapter will be subjective and, at times, controversial, I want to stress that all my opinions are based on reading mountains of stories – thousands and thousands over the years. Some have impressed me, some have baffled me, and others have made me scream in frustration!

So this is my own personal view of things. Of course, I'd be delighted if you wanted to embrace my likes and dislikes, and perhaps use this insider knowledge to help you do well in any comp I'm judging.

If, however, you intend to steer clear of any competition I'm involved with (and who can blame you!) and want to disagree with some of the points I make, feel free. Merely take in any useful competition winning information from this section and ignore the rest ... and thank your lucky stars that judges aren't all the same!

Tell it to the judge

I hope you'll indulge me for a few moments. I think it would be useful if I told you a bit about myself. After all, I'm laying down the law and advising you on how to think and act so you're entitled to ask: *just who do you think you are?*

Well, for one thing I'm a competitions nut – I just can't get enough of them. Very early in my career I won a couple of prizes for my short stories and that did it – I was hooked.

It only takes someone to mention a writing comp – even if he's whispering three rooms away – and my ears prick up and I stop in mid stride. I get that excited tingle and I'm instantly rushing to my computer to start knocking out lists of possible plots ... and that's before I've even heard what genre it's aimed at or what the prize is.

You name it, I've done it – spent a week's wages on entries to win a comp offering just a modest book token; submitted more than a dozen stories to a single contest; tried to enter so many events simultaneously that I've been up in the small hours night after night frantically writing. And that's just the things I can admit to.

Luckily, I've won enough prizes over the years to justify my addiction and convince my wife not to divorce me – although it's been a near thing on occasions!

So, don't worry – there's nothing you can tell me about this game that I won't have heard before or that will shock me. I've been there, done that, got the therapy.

In my other persona I've been judging for what seems like a lifetime and a half. But I certainly didn't set out to become a competition adjudicator. I didn't plan it. It wasn't on my list of career objectives. It just sort of happened ...

There were a variety of different reasons why I ended up judging. Firstly, my success in various comps brought me to the attention of organisers and I was asked if I'd like to see what life was like "on the other side of the fence". I thought: *why not? This might be fun. And even if it isn't, I'll get the chance to see the mistakes others make and learn to avoid them in my own work.*

In addition, my stories started to appear regularly in magazines, and as a result writers' groups were keen to book me as a speaker revealing my secrets of impressing fiction editors. Several groups said: *why not judge our annual comp as well while you're at it.*

Then the correspondence school I tutored for asked me to judge their annual national competition several years in a row, and this led to other groups approaching me to adjudicate their contests.

And lastly (and this doesn't paint me in a very good light) I sat down and did my sums. I realised the simple mercenary truth that although I enjoyed the uncertainty and tension of not knowing whether I was going to win anything, there was a small part of me that rather liked the idea of getting a cheque for every competition I was involved with – and the only way to guarantee that was to be the judge.

So, in the last few years, I have to admit that I've switched a bit from someone crazy about entering as many competitions as possible to being someone crazy about judging as many competitions as possible.

What will turn my head?

Okay, that's enough of the family history lecture. Let's get on to the meat.

What type of stories do I like? What is going to make me sit up and take notice? What is the secret of short story success? Just what is going to make someone as jaundiced and grouchy as me award a prize?

There is no simple answer. Or certainly there's no easy "one-size-fits-all" formula that is guaranteed to snatch the glittering trophies. I see great yarns of different types, written in a multiplicity of diverse styles, all of which make me purr with pleasure. I'm thrilled by writers who tackle the task of storytelling in bold and unorthodox ways.

There's nothing remotely similar about them – except perhaps that they are all masterly. They are a cut above the crowd. That doesn't just mean that they stand out through the sheer technical skill and creativity of the author. It means that each story is unique. It has its own fresh slant on life.

Often the writers are providing a razor-sharp insight into human nature. They understand people and what makes us all tick. They show us at our best and our worst. They show us people with flaws and admirable qualities – characters we can empathise with, characters we can imagine ourselves meeting in real life, characters we can care about.

I especially like narratives which wield a strong emotional punch. I feel moved when I read them. Whether I'm crying, recoiling in horror or just smiling ruefully, I experience an emotional response to events in the story. It's not just a plot and a few clever twists, it's a tale that has something to say and the writer knows how to make it shout that message.

Nothing is so impressive as a story that works on several levels, where there is sub-text and layers of meaning. In a magazine story this isn't necessary. Often it isn't possible. The magazine writer usually can't indulge in nuance and subtlety, but in a competition this kind of "texturing" is what a judge looks for, what makes a story something special.

It's what the strained silences between the characters are revealing that matters. These awkward gaps tell us as much about the characters' relationship and feelings as the things they say or do.

It's the words that often go unspoken which speak the loudest ... *oh why didn't he tell her he loved her? She's walking out through the door. Three little words could stop his life being ruined* ...

Or it's the meaning lying just below the surface of their dialogue that tells us what is really going on. The teacher verbally tears the pupil's work to pieces. But we know it's not because she is bad at her work, but because he has secret sexual desires towards her and fears anyone finding out about his attraction. The more he dismisses her efforts, the safer he feels ... but the reader knows the truth.

Perhaps the story is being told from an unusual viewpoint:

- An adult row is being observed by a child who fails to understand why her parents are arguing.

- The boardroom take-over is seen not through the eyes of the managing director losing everything but through the eyes of the charwoman he has always ill-treated.

- The execution is observed from the perspective of the repair man called in at the last minute to fix the faulty electric chair. It was only a job to him, like any other – until he sees the condemned man being strapped in. But now he feels revulsion, directed at the guards, but mostly towards himself.

Or it tells the story from the perspective of someone who we would never usually expect to be a narrator. Perhaps, for example, the serpent relating the narrative of Adam and Eve's expulsion from Eden and his part in engineering their downfall.

And what about an unexpected "angle"? How about the serpent expressing remorse and saying it was all a mistake. History has got his role in the affair all wrong and he wants to put the record straight!

From the last example, you can probably guess that I like stories with a surreal edge, especially funny stories with a surreal edge. Humour is a really welcome element to any judge faced with a tower block of scripts to read through.

I know that I always give thanks for those writers who've used a light and funny touch in their storytelling. It helps to add a pinch of sparkle in what is often a pile of doom-laden, dark and ultimately depressing tales of greed, murder and mayhem.

The humour has to be clever, though. I don't like slapstick, sub-standard silliness or juvenile puns, but if I can find a writer who makes me smile while at the same time using the story to put across a serious point, then his writing will be guaranteed to be selected for the shortlist.

But I don't only choose funny stories. These are only one type of narrative goodie in the huge smorgasbord of styles, settings and plots that will appeal to me. All sorts of stories make me go: *Wow, I wish I'd written that!* You'll get to read some of them in Chapter Twelve.

Plot, what plot?

Perhaps it would be easier if I explained what I'm not looking for. What I dread seeing.

One of my biggest bugbears is writers who have submitted stories that have no plot – or a plot so thin and weak that it threatens to snap at any moment. They fail to realise that carefully crafted character sketches or lengthy passages of colourful, lyrical scene setting are no substitute for plot.

A short story is exactly what it says on the tin: a story. It must have a narrative. Events must take place. Characters must meet, talk, interact, clash, change each other's lives. Something must happen – there must be drama, tension and suspense.

A short story isn't the place to paint static word pictures, to construct immobile tableaux. A story needs movement, and plenty of it.

It's the place to tell us all about the unusual occurrences that startlingly disrupt your main character's life, turning it upside down and forcing him to face a problem or dilemma. We follow him as he hurtles headlong towards a solution to the conflict which is plaguing him.

Culprits usually submit pieces which are really just writing exercises, colour pieces which describe what various people and buildings look like in some village or town. They never go beyond creating this scenic backdrop. There's no room for plot – or they never bother to dream one up.

Other writers provide the basic "set-up" of a narrative but never develop it into a fully fledged plot. They don't realise that an attention grabbing set-up is vital but it's what happens later, the incidents that flare up from this initial dramatic spark, that actually make the story.

Having two people who hate each other's guts share a flat is a great basic set-up – it's packed with potential drama – but it's not the story. The plot is actually what they get up to once they've moved in! These conflict-laden incidents are the plot. The story line is the chain of events that eventually brings them to the point where they ... bury the hatchet ... kill each other ... move out ... fall in love ...

It's important that you understand the difference between a set-up and a plot. Think of a story as a journey. It must go somewhere. The set-up is merely the point at which you board the train.

Doomed to fail

If pressed to give one single reason why most stories fail in competition I would say it's because they are formula twist-enders which, although competently written, offer nothing new or exciting. There's nothing hugely wrong with them, they work perfectly well, but they lack sparkle and pizzazz – and, above all, originality.

I can tell that they were originally penned for a popular (usually women's) magazine and have failed to find a home. The author is trying them in competition as a last resort.

These yarns never make it on to the shortlist. It's not surprising when you stop to think about it. As a judge I want a story that is different, that stands out, something unique. A fiction editor, more often than not, is looking for something mass-produced – a standard yarn told in the third person with three middle-class characters, a 1000-word length, domestic setting, a woman as main character and the "sting" in the last six words.

I'm looking for an individualistic voice and vision. Fiction editors seek stories that are similar in tone and style to those they always print. They know their readers and provide what they want. Your work can't please both of us – it's just not possible.

Of course, because these entries were really written for the magazine market the plots are always variations on the same theme – the wronged woman who puts one over on the man who has treated her unfairly or harshly. The worm turns ... and turns ... and turns ...

This may – just possibly – be why men seem to do so well in short story contests. It's not that judges are biased (you've already heard my protestations on that point in Chapter Five) but because male writers sit down and write a fresh story **specially** for the competition.

They don't start with any preconceptions, fettered by the conventions and restrictions of a particular market. They just get on with telling a good story in whatever happens to be their natural style.

Now, I know this is a controversial point of view and I may be wrong, but it's certainly worth thinking about – isn't it?

Regardless of whether this is a gender point, I am sure that the fact that much of the published short fiction we all see is in supermarket checkout magazines accounts for why so many competitors limit themselves to settings that are contemporary, commonplace and cosy. That is what fiction editors demand – settings that readers can easily recognise, and feel at home in. But it's not what a competition judge wants to see.

I yearn for colourful, rich, luxurious stories set in exotic and astonishing locations – stories set in different eras and worlds. I long to read work where a free spirit has woven a magical narrative spell, using their storytelling and descriptive powers to the full. Someone ready to take me someplace I've never been before; someplace where anything can happen ... and probably will. Nondescript office worker Chloe plotting revenge against the boss who passed her over for promotion just isn't going to do it!

Chestnuts roasting on an open fire

Something else that will kill a yarn's chances is a hackneyed story line. It's amazing how often the same sorry chestnut plots come round. You can't really blame judges for getting a little jaundiced when they see them, grumpily feeling that most competitors are hopelessly devoid of imagination.

I've lost count of the stories I have read featuring the old clichés of people planning murder who are themselves killed by their intended prey or con-men who are taken to the cleaners by their potential victims. These over-familiar stories never win prizes – why should they?

And that's before we even start looking at all the other predictable retreads – the sting in the tail stories where the narrator turns out to be a cat, dog, budgie or hamster (all miraculously able to use a word processor); the twist-ender where the flaming passion of two starry lovers turns out to be between five-year-olds and the horror stories in which the narrator turns out to be a werewolf, vampire, Frankenstein monster, ghoul, or Jack The Ripper.

These are matched by the sci-fi stories which deal with the now tedious theme of superpower nuclear war – especially those post holocaust yarns where the last two survivors are (surprise, surprise) called Adam and Eve.

I'm particularly turned off by so called spooky stories where it's yet another haunted house, haunted mirror, haunted computer (used perhaps by a ghost writer?), haunted portrait or haunted car. Some people manage to compound the crime by having a murderer killed by the ghost of his victim – two clichés for the price of one! This is one genre that's been done to death (sorry about the pun). My advice is to avoid this area altogether unless the competition specifically asks for ghost stories. If it does, please don't ask me to judge it.

The worst ghost story chestnut is the motorist who breaks down late at night outside a picturesque country cottage. A kindly old woman takes pity on him and gives him shelter from the storm. After eating a scrumptious home-cooked meal, the motorist sinks into a dreamless sleep in a warm feather bed.

He wakes in the cold light of dawn to find that the cottage has either become dilapidated or vanished altogether. When he asks in the village he's told that no-one lived there for years, not since apple-cheeked Granny Smith died.

Oh dear. How many times have I read a version of this? Hardly a competition goes by without this corny story line featuring somewhere in the entry pile.

Four other story lines pop up with regular monotony. The first of these is the middle aged care assistant at the nursing home who realises that the old person who has just been admitted is the teacher who used to torment and terrify her when she was a girl, or the boss who treated her badly when she used to work for him.

He doesn't recognise her but she angrily remembers all the ill-treatment she suffered at his hands. The question is: will she get her revenge, or will she take pity on him in his frail, helpless, senile state?

The next is the story of Helen's big wedding day. It usually describes her radiant glow, the gorgeous dress, how proud her father is, all the fuss and commotion with her at the centre of it. The twist here is that Helen isn't the bride – she's the eight-year-old bridesmaid!

Then there's the story where the woman narrator is so in love with the new man she's just met. She's planning a life of bliss with him until she's shocked and saddened to see her man in the street, hugging another female. How could he? The two-timer!

I bet you've already guessed it. Yes, the woman that he's hugging is actually his sister. It's all above board. Naturally, this is a sister that the narrator has conveniently never met or even heard about. Groan ...

The last of this quaint quartet is the tale dealing with the husband who is acting strangely. He disappears from the house without explanation, seems to be distracted and makes furtive phone calls which convince his wife that he's having an affair.

She's mortified when she follows him to the home of her best friend. Oh the betrayal! But wait – it's not what it seems. The husband isn't two-timing her – quite the opposite. He's been secretly planning a 25th wedding anniversary party. The best friend has been helping out. That's what all the phone calls and meetings have been about – they've been making the arrangements.

It is difficult not to sigh loudly when these shop-worn horrors raise their ugly heads. But still people keep submitting them. Please make it your business to learn the hackneyed plots and avoid them. Not only will it increase your chances of winning, it will make this battle-scarred judge a little less depressed.

Pet hates

Okay, we've established that I hate cliché plots, but what else is guaranteed to turn me off? Well, duff intros are a particular pet hate.

These are stories that start with a few lines of vague dialogue with nothing to explain who is talking, what they are talking about, where they are at the time, exactly who they are talking to or what their relationship is to one another.

I read and reread the opening lines trying to figure out what's going on, and fail miserably. It's all just a big muddle. The writer obviously knows but he's determined he's not going to share the knowledge with us. He'd rather be cryptic – in a mistaken attempt to be mysterious or atmospheric.

It may take half a page before things start to become clear. But, by that time I've lost interest. I don't care anymore. I'm already mentally thinking: *next please ...*

Then there are the intros where the author is determined to give me a lecture before the story starts. Instead of starting with a dramatic, attention-grabbing incident to get the story off and running, he spends the opening half page describing the location where the action is going to eventually take place, or describing the main character and his background.

The effect is a bit like going to the theatre and finding that the director won't let the curtains open until he's come out to speak to the audience and told us absolutely everything about the characters we'll meet.

You'd think it odd in a play, so why do it in a short story? Don't set the scene. Don't give a briefing on the hero's life-story and aspirations. Get going! Give us all that information later (if it's really necessary) as the plot unfolds.

A favourite with some writers is the boring, pensive, "woman staring out of the window" opening. As the heroine gazes out across the countryside she mulls over the unexpected and terrible events that have brought her to this point. She ponders what to do.

Her thoughts wander through the past, undisturbed except by the noise of the judge snoring loudly over the manuscript. And you can't blame him because, no matter how you dress it up, a single person sitting silently in a room is a big yawn. It's dull, static and unengaging.

The idea is to immediately catch and then hold the judge's interest. And, like all readers, he wants something exciting to happen – movement, speech, character inter-action, drama, tension, suspense, conflict, confrontation, dilemma, danger ... anything but gentle musings.

Never have an opening like this. The easy solution is to always start with two people talking – preferably having a row.

If lots of people have trouble with their openings, just as many seem to stumble over their story endings. They seem unable to bring a story to a short, sharp, satisfying conclusion. They either fail to create a climax, or stop too abruptly for no apparent reason.

Your story should – like a good joke – end on a punch-line. It should end the moment that the dilemma or problem that was plaguing your main character is resolved. The denouement should elicit an emotional response from the reader – even if it's just a loud groan from a bad joke.

It really saddens me when I'm enjoying a story and start to think: *yes, this one's in with a good shout* and then a weak ending lets it down. I have a profound sense of disappointment – and irritation – that, having done all the hard work, the competitor has thrown it away at the final hurdle.

Some endings are so crass that they make me want to put my head in my hands and weep. Often the writer's concocted an illogical and unbelievable finale that hasn't evolved from the events that have gone before, and which seems to have been grafted on from an entirely different tale.

For example, two con-men visit an old granny posing as workmen. They intend to swindle her out of her life savings, pretending to have carried out urgently needed repairs to her roof. Distressed and confused, she hands over the cash.

They drive away laughing but their joy doesn't last for long because they are ... involved in a smash with a double decker bus/abducted by aliens/attacked by a vampire that has been hiding in their van/arrested by an armed police response team that has set up road blocks to catch a gang of bank robbers and fortuitously gets the con-men instead. And so on ...

Other awful endings are where really weird things happen in a story – impossible, improbable things – and you can see the writer slowly tying himself into narrative knots. There's no way he can successfully resolve it all with a logical or credible ending so he presses the "escape" button and writes: *And then I woke up and it was all a dream.* Ahhh!!!

Do me a favour. This juvenile cop-out isn't an acceptable ending to a school essay, never mind a competition story.

The other ending that is guaranteed to insult the reader's intelligence is: *Sorry, I can't write any more. The men in white coats are coming round with my medication.*

Yeah, right. We're supposed to think this story is deep and ponder whether the surreal events described really happened or whether they are just the fevered imaginings of a disturbed mind. Well I don't know and, moreover, I don't care.

Almost as infuriating are what I call Fairy Godmother endings. That's where the hero's life just gets worse and worse. Everything that can go wrong, does. He loses his job, the bills pile up, the landlord is about to evict him, his wife is about to walk out and he contemplates suicide, but unexpectedly help arrives on the last page in the shape of: a lottery win/an uncle dying in Australia and leaving him a sheep farm/an old school friend bumping into him in the street and offering him a super new job/his old boss having a change of heart and re-employing him with a nice juicy wage rise/a genie popping up with the obligatory three wishes ...

He gets off the hook easily – not through his own ingenuity, hard work and guts, but through the writer acting as a Fairy Godmother and conveniently plucking him from danger.

Apart from the fact that life isn't like that, this approach to storytelling shows nothing but contempt for the reader. We've been tricked into caring what happened to this guy, being concerned for him – but, hey, he was never in any real peril. It was all a con. We were duped.

Other turn-offs

I always feel my heart sink when I start to read a story where the characters have no names.

As "the man" rushes to meet "the woman" my attention rushes to ... what I'm having for lunch. Sorry, but I just can't generate any interest in nameless people. They aren't proper characters, real people – just symbols, two-dimensional chess pieces being moved around the story.

There's nothing to bring me closer to them, or create any sort of empathy. Nameless people remain forever strangers. I don't care about strangers, only people I know.

I'm always suspicious of writers who don't give names to their characters. I'm convinced they either haven't put enough creative time and effort into the story or can't visualise what their characters should look like or what their personalities are. And if the writer himself can't get a mental image, how on earth are we supposed to?

Usually stories that have nameless characters also suffer from a lack of other descriptive material. Nothing is adequately drawn ... not the atmosphere, the setting, the weather, the time of day. It's all a bit fuzzy. The reader has no clues, nothing to help him build a picture in his mind.

I also dislike "first person" stories where the gender of the narrator is unclear and I have to wait until half way down page three to know whether I'm reading about a man or a woman. It's irritating (and sloppy) when the writer says: *I did this/I went there/I cried with joy* and it isn't obvious from the text whether the "I" main character is male or female.

As well as making it impossible to picture the story-teller, it can make the yarn difficult to follow and, in some cases, unintentionally funny.

The words: *I struggled into my tights* suggest that it's a woman, but hang on a minute – what if it's a male ballet dancer? What if it's an otherwise respectable man who has a guilty secret, and cold legs? See what confusion this ambiguity causes?

Always make sure that you find some way of signalling to the reader which sex your main character is ... *the boss looks at me threateningly but I'm determined to show him I'm a man who doesn't back down.*

Other pet hates? Plagiarism (I'll talk about that later) and stories written merely to let the author show off how devastatingly witty, clever and erudite he is. I find these particularly irksome.

We all like to think we're smart and a cut above the herd but that's no excuse for going off on a massive ego trip. Stick to telling the story. That's all that matters. It's a storytelling competition not a superiority complex demonstration. All the judge cares about is whether you can weave a narrative that enthrals and entertains.

Personally, I'm unmoved by the fact that you're well read and like to drop the names of 19th century French philosophers into the text, have a classical education and can make allusions to obscure Greek gods or have the largest vocabulary in the universe and can spout six syllable words like a verbal machine gun.

I am also unimpressed by competitors who believe that writing is an exercise in "word painting" and should consist of overblown images, baroque, flowery expressions and purple prose.

Beam me up Scottie

I've heard it said that it isn't worth entering a sci-fi or fantasy story in a competition because they aren't treated fairly. Sadly, I suspect there is more than a grain of truth in this. No-one ever admits it, but if you mention robots, time travel and space exploration to most judges, you can spot the merest flicker of amusement in their eyes, the slight – just perceptible – curl of the lip.

It upsets me that sci-fi is still seen as a second-class ghetto genre which suffers from a great deal of intellectual snobbery, especially as I don't share this prejudice. I love stories with an alien or futuristic setting. I was brought up on the short stories of legends like Isaac Asimov, Bob Shaw and Robert Heinlein, and spent countless hours glued to the TV screen watching *Star Trek*, *Lost in Space* and *Doctor Who*.

But, despite being a sci-fi fanatic, I have to be honest and admit that I can't remember ever having given a prize to a science fiction story. It's not because I'm biased. It's not a pet hate. Nothing would give me a bigger thrill than to award first prize to some transwarp, intergalactic, space-suited tale. But the stories people enter just aren't up to it. In fact, most are boring and formulaic, and the rest are just plain embarrassing.

The big problem is that writers just can't seem to come up with anything new. Everything feels like a rehash of the shop-worn themes, settings and characters. Some competitors are so openly derivative that I can pick the story to pieces, labelling where every element has been lifted from – that's the invisible rampaging monster from *Predator*; rebels fighting on the ice planet from *The Empire Strikes Back*; the terrorised colonists from *Aliens*; the amusingly *Enterprising* android who wants to be human ...

Whether these writers are knowingly being magpies and imagine that no-one will spot that they're ripping off famous films and TV shows, or are doing this subconsciously and innocently, the end result is still the same. I go through each story thinking: haven't I seen this basic set-up before, a hundred times? Where's the spark of originality? Can people do nothing except send in retreads?

Others fail because they produce work that is unintentionally camp – with death rays, bug-eyed monsters and men dressed in tights or oven-ready silver-foil costumes. Such yarns frequently feature people with silly names – always starting with Z – such as Zudos, Zug, Zephan, Zebedie, Zaron. Or they have strange titles like *Guardian of the Inner Wisdom* or *Second Prelate of the Galactic Alliance*. These romps are more *Flash Gordon* than *2001*.

Some over-ambitious souls fall into the trap of having long, convoluted narratives – trying to cram a novel's worth of involved plot into a short story. Instead, they end up with a disjointed muddle. They'd be better remembering the basic rules of short storytelling: keep it short, keep it simple. Stick to one narrative thread.

Many forget that science fiction should be about people and relationships and devote half of the story to stultifyingly dull descriptions of revolutionary rocket drives.

Sometimes it seems like this genre is hexed, cursed forever to attract people who can't write or are devoid of fresh ideas. Even as a fan it's hard to take this kind of thing seriously. This is a shame, as I would love to read some well-written, thought-provoking sci-fi entries.

Do judges cut corners?

I am often asked if I actually read all the way through the entries I receive. Surely I can tell a stinker right from the first page? Why waste my time reading further, especially as I know from long experience that it's unheard of for a story to start badly then miraculously improve later on?

Well, I have to admit that it can be tempting not to wade all the way through an obviously hopeless story, particularly when there's a huge pile of entries looming ominously in the corner and organisers are demanding a quick turn around.

But, although it's an enticing thought to immediately junk a "no-hoper" I always fight to resist that siren call to cut corners. I live in the naïve hope that one day I will find that mythical one-in-a-million story that does have a knock-em-dead ending that makes up for a terrible, lacklustre opening.

I also have a slightly loftier reason for sticking with stories. I tell myself that no matter how badly a yarn reads, the writer paid the same entry fee as everyone else and his story deserves exactly the same amount of time and consideration.

In fact, at the risk of sounding too priggish, I look upon it as a point of honour that I don't short-change competitors. Writing is a difficult game and anyone who has a go, even if he does it badly, deserves respect. And entry fees certainly aren't cheap these days!

Besides, I can still remember what it was like to be a competitor and I would have been furious if I thought for a moment that the judge hadn't read my masterpiece all the way through.

I can't speak for all judges, of course, but I don't know anyone else who cuts corners. So don't worry. You can be fairly confident that your work gets full, detailed scrutiny.

If you are concerned, always target a competition where the entries receive a comprehensive critique. If the judge has to comment on the climax of the story it ensures he reads it to the end!

Of course, you could just make sure your opening is a stunner and seductively lures the reader into the narrative and won't let go ...

The judging process

Well, having established that I read the stories all the way through, this is probably a good point to explain how I go about selecting the winners.

Judges all have their own ways of tackling the task but as I go through the judging bundle I always separate the stories into four piles:

- For immediate disqualification
- Hopeless
- Okay, but nothing special
- Dazzling

The stories that go into the disqualification pile are the ones where the writer has obviously broken or ignored the rules.

These will be entries that are hand-written when the rules insist on typed; material that greatly exceeds the maximum word limit (no matter what the writer may optimistically claim on the title sheet); entries that aren't short stories but songs, poems or articles; work that isn't set out in double line spacing; work so faintly printed that it is illegible and entries that proudly bear the author's name, address and phone number – clearly identifying the competitor.

Others immediately disqualified will be entries that have broken competition etiquette – obvious rip-offs, those which I recognise from last year's competition, and any which I have previously given prizes to in this or some other comp and hence I know aren't eligible.

I also weed out those pieces which aren't set out in the manner requested on the entry form. This last point may sound harsh, but I know from years of experience that no story of any merit arrives single-spaced, on yellowing paper, faintly printed and covered in coffee stains.

Competitors who are slipshod about presentation are always slipshod about the actual writing as well.

Next, I look to weed out the "stinkers". These are the really badly written stories, which are quickly consigned to the hopeless pile. Depressingly, they make up the majority of entries in most competitions. These are entries where the writer's basic storytelling skills aren't up to it, or the use of English is so poor that it seriously mars the work.

It's a sad fact of life that wanting to be a writer doesn't automatically equip you with the talent or the skills, and I often see work where the writer doesn't have any grasp of the techniques necessary to turn out a logically structured, coherent and engaging piece of fiction.

Competitions are enormous fun to enter, but they aren't really the place to send your work if you're an absolute novice, find writing a struggle or can't get into print.

If anything, the standard is higher than you'd normally expect for any magazine and you have to bear that in mind.

But what about the rest, the stories that **are** well written? Well, any entry that reads engagingly but is too formulaic or fails to excite me goes into the "nothing special" pile. These are usually by people who have the ability to write with confidence and precision, but haven't quite got enough originality. With the right prodding and coaching, they would turn out sizzling material but they don't take enough risks. They play too safe. Their work lacks flair.

And for writers who do have that special something, whose work has flair, freshness and impact? They are the entries that I put in my "dazzling" pile – the stars, the stories that thrill, inspire, stimulate and provoke. These are the super yarns that will battle it out for ultimate glory.

Second reading

If things work well, there will be enough good yarns in the "dazzling" pile to provide me with a sizeable and varied short-list for the "second reading" phase. If not, if I have less than 20 stories, I'll go back to the "just okay" pile and promote the best two or three to the first division. I then make my final selection from this revised shortlist pile.

This may seem an over-elaborate way to make choices. Why not just have two piles – good and bad? Or why not just pluck the winners straight out of the mass of stories as I read?

The truth is that in the middle of scanning 500 or more short stories anyone's judgement will become a bit numbed. It becomes difficult to tell whether a story you've just read is truly good or just average. There are usually so many poor quality entries that when I do encounter a decent story I immediately fall in love with it. I almost cheer with relief. At last someone who knows what they're doing!

But although it's undoubtedly a good story, it's probably not that remarkable or memorable when I read it again later, in a cooler frame of mind. The story leapt out at me initially because the others around it were so dull. It remains a competent and well constructed narrative, of course, but not an outstanding story deserving a prize.

I find this fresh and more objective second look relegates quite a few entries to the "okay, but nothing special" pile.

Tipped for the top

In reality, finding the best five stories in any competition is easy – they'll usually choose themselves. They will excel. They will be: professionally constructed, lyrically written, clever, moving – obvious champions. The difficult part of the process is choosing which comes first, which gets second place, which is placed third and so on.

Each story will be a great read, engagingly written and memorable. All will be the cream. But how to decide between them? How do you pick the lucky person who is going to be the outright winner and get that first prize rosette? That's when the adjudicator's skill, experience, careful judgement – and prejudices – come into it.

I've always found writing from a child's viewpoint to be extremely tricky to get right, and I'm always full of admiration for writers who make it look easy. So in the last few years I've selected quite a number of stories where the events are seen through the eyes of a child.

It wasn't a conscious decision on my part. It wasn't a bias I was aware of, but it's a trend in my thinking I've just spotted recently. Whether I'll choose any more child-view stories in future, now that I'm aware of it, I can't say.

I'm sure other judges all have their own subconscious likes and dislikes. So, up to a point, it's a matter of luck whether having made the final handful of winners, you end up getting first place or third.

And it gets even worse when the judge has a committee "helping" him. Sometimes an adjudicator will be instructed to pick the best ten stories and make recommendations on which **might** be the top three but the final, binding selection from his shortlist is down to the committee. That's when the fun begins!

Luckily, I haven't often found myself in this position as a judge, but I did suffer as a competitor years ago. I came third in a major national competition. I was quite happy with this, as the prestige in getting a prize of any sort was huge.

I was content ... until the judge, a best-selling novelist, had a few drinks with me over the presentation lunch and let slip that he'd really wanted me to come first but there'd been a big row with some members of the organising committee. They'd wanted a story that was more "literary" and less "commercial" to get the main prize. Unfortunately, the committee – none of whom were writers – won out. Shame.

Shortlist glory

In most competitions getting to the shortlist is an achievement in itself. You've beaten hundreds of other writers, some of whom will be much more experienced than you are. And I believe people should know that they've done well – even if they haven't actually made it over the final hurdle into the prizes.

That's why I always ask organisers to tell everyone on the shortlist that they succeeded in getting to the second reading phase. It doesn't cost anything, and I feel it's worth making the gesture because of the huge amount of excitement, satisfaction and goodwill it generates. After all, it can be hard enough in this game to get any kind of meaningful feedback and this tips the wink to writers that they are on the right track.

Grammar grumps

There's one last point worth making about the judging process. And that's the fact that I believe strongly that good grammar, syntax and spelling are important in a competition.

It always influences my decision when I see a piece that is littered with silly spelling mistakes, is incorrectly punctuated, or has sentences so clumsily constructed that they are cryptic or ambiguous.

I'm sorry if this sounds harsh but I feel a writer should be in total control of language. It's a basic prerequisite of the job. Creating a dramatic narrative is great, but you must be able to use English properly. Your meaning must always be clear.

I wouldn't disqualify anyone for bad spelling or erratic punctuation, but it would be a deciding factor in making my final selection between two equally matched stories.

So always check through your work thoroughly, and get a friend to look through it too. Winning competitions is all about making a good impression. Don't allow anything in your story to detract from the story's impact.

Plagiarism: a cautionary tale

Now, I'd like to end this in-depth look at short story comps by talking a little about plagiarism. In Chapter Four we warned against the dangers of lifting someone else's work and trying to pass it off as your own. You would, we promised, get caught.

And just to prove it, here's a blatant example of theft that I came across in a recent short story competition. I won't name the culprit or the comp involved. Although he doesn't deserve it, I will spare the writer's blushes!

This competitor thought he was being clever by "borrowing" his story line from a fairly obscure album track by American folk singer Harry Chapin.

The song is called "Taxi" and, coincidentally, so was this writer's entry. The Chapin song tells the story of what happens when a disillusioned San Francisco taxi driver stops to pick up a fare and realises that the rich woman is a former girlfriend.

He reminisces bitterly about their lost love and their broken dreams. He'd intended to become a pilot and she was going to be an actress but things hadn't worked out for either of them.

They make awkward small talk and he drops her off at her mansion. She says they must get together some time but they both know she doesn't mean it.

It's a poignant song, packed with meaning, but it's one that few people would have heard of. That's not surprising as Harry Chapin died some 20 years ago. But as luck would have it, I'm a Harry Chapin fanatic – I have virtually every track he ever recorded.

So imagine my delight when I started to read this short story – now switched to a British setting – about a mini-cab driver who picks up a woman passenger and as he drives her to her posh house he realises that they used to be sweethearts.

He reminisces bitterly about their lost love and their broken dreams. He'd intended to become a doctor and she was going to go to business college, but things hadn't worked out for either of them.

They make awkward small talk and she says they must get together some time but they both realise she doesn't really mean it ... ring any bells?

Now, I instantly disqualified this rip-off. The writer had even directly lifted lines of lyric and used them word for word. What cheek!

But the biting irony of this incident is that the original song – written back in the 1960s – has the woman giving the driver a $20 note for a $2.50 fare and telling him to keep the change. He has so little self respect left that he gladly takes this handout.

In our writer's cut-price modernised copy, the woman gives the driver just a £10 note for an £8 fare and tells him to keep the change. Suddenly this pivotal "charity" gesture has been robbed of all meaning or impact.

If the woman gives the cabbie a tip that is **eight times** the fare it speaks volumes about the guilt she feels. It is a telling insight into how their relative status has forever changed. But for her merely to give a cabbie a 20 per cent tip is no big deal. It has no sub-text or special significance. It says nothing.

To nick someone else's work is despicable, but to steal a piece and fail to understand the dynamics of what makes it work in the first place ... well, words fail me!

Anyway, enough of me preaching. Back to the moral of this story. No matter how clever you think you are, and how old or obscure the work you rip off, Sod's Law dictates that the judge will be the only other person in the world who's heard of it. Don't take the risk.

8

THE WORLD OF
POETRY COMPETITIONS

In the last chapter Iain came clean about his fascination with short story comps, addiction to the whole competition scene, and what turns him off – and on – when he's adjudicating. Now it's my turn, and I want to explain how I go about the judging process, offer a few chunks of general advice and share my personal thoughts about poetry comps.

Remember, you're only getting the reflections of one of the many judges who are working on poetry competitions; but my views are formed from reading a few thousand poems a year, many of which are brilliant and make me wish I'd written them, but many more of which make we wonder how anybody believes they stand a snowball's chance in hell of winning a prize.

Like Iain, I'll use the first person throughout this chapter, and like him, I'll introduce myself first. Forgive me if you think you've already read this first bit, though, because much of my experience of poetry competitions is similar to Iain's with prose contests.

It took me a while to discover that there were actually competitions for writing poetry, and by the time I found them I was enjoying just a little success with publication in small press magazines, and my first "slim vol" of poetry had been unleashed on an unsuspecting public which would probably have been a lot happier without it.

A chance encounter with an actor outside the Royal Shakespeare Theatre during which about eight words were exchanged gave me the idea for a poem, and while I was still working on it I heard about a literary festival competition, and decided to try my luck. I won a £5 book token. Heady stuff! I drove more than 200 miles through the night to collect it. And I was hooked.

After that, I entered every competition that was going. My husband and daughters rapidly learned to cook, clean and do all the other things I couldn't do because I was finishing a poem for a competition, dashing to catch the last post with an entry, working out the sums to ensure that I could keep to my self-appointed quota without breaking the bank, or poring over an anthology of prize winners.

Needless to say, most of my efforts sank without trace, but that didn't dampen my enthusiasm. I collected entry forms from the library, arts centre and meetings of the local writers' circle, and if anyone used the "c" word in my hearing I badgered them for all the details. I had enough wins to keep my interest alive, and gradually enough success to be able to indulge the long-suffering family a bit – to compensate for all that cooking and cleaning they'd had to do.

When a writers' group where I was giving a poetry reading asked me to judge their next internal competition, I floated on clouds for days. I must have spent every spare minute in the next month making my decision, which is curious because there were only about twelve entries. They, too, gave me a book token as a "thank you", and it suddenly struck me that being a judge meant you got to read all the poems, had a brief taste of omnipotence, and even got paid.

As soon as you have adjudicated one competition, people start asking you to do more. I loved adjudicating so much that I made a point of never turning down a request to judge anything if I could possible take it on, and I'm still steadfastly refusing to say no.

I am always being asked what I look for in a poetry competition, and although the answer may seem like a cop-out, I honestly can't say what I want to find until I find it. I'm looking for a poem that will send a tingle down my spine, make my face go numb, force me to read it a dozen times. I'm looking for a poem that will grab my attention and keep distracting me from the other things in my life by drawing me back for days after I first read it.

When I'm judging an open competition the winning poem could be in any form, rhymed or unrhymed, metrical or non-metrical, humorous, weighty, lyrical, narrative – anything. But it must be good, brilliant, original, fantastic. If the competition requires a poem in a set form, it must adhere to the form absolutely. If it specifies a theme, that theme must be treated from a new and exciting angle, or in an unexpected or powerful way.

In short, I'm looking for the perfect poem – the one I wish I'd written myself.

Picking the winner

So how do I go about finding the poem with the x-factor, tingle potential? I start not with words but with numbers. I open the parcel(s) of entries, and count the poems into groups of fifty, and check exactly how many there are altogether. I find it helpful to know at any time roughly what proportion of the entries I've read, and I can see that at a glance by noting the number of piles of fifty remaining. Fifty is significant – I often look at fewer but never read more than fifty poems at a stretch, because I know that's my limit. If I read any more, I can feel my attention beginning to wander, and that mustn't be allowed to happen under any circumstances.

I read every word of every poem. Iain explained the reason for this perfectly, by pointing out that even the competitor whose manuscript shows the least promise has paid the same fee as everyone else, and so deserves the same respect and courtesy.

At this first reading I reject all those poems exhibiting obvious flaws, and retain the fantastic, the hopeful and the "well, it's got something going for it". I re-read these, preferably a good few days after the completion of the first trawl. At this stage, the hopeful and the "well, its got something ... " have to depart, leaving only the fantastic. This usually leaves me with about a tenth of the original entry.

I read these many more times, both silently and aloud, at different times of the day, even in different rooms in my house. I want to ensure that every poem has a fair chance, and is read as impartially as possible, whatever its content. I gradually – and regretfully – shed entries from this longer shortlist until I reach the final shortlist of winners, highly commendeds etc. These are shuffled about physically – usually all over the living room floor – and mentally until the winner emerges.

Occasionally a winner will leap from the pile during the initial trawl, tell me it deserves first prize, and go on to win that prize. It still has to go through all the processes, though, to make certain that it lives up to its first impressions.

It really hurts to have to drop those poems which are near misses – the ones that might have won with a different judge, or that could have been successful if the competition had not been contested so hotly. But it has to be done – that's what I get paid for. So I say goodbye and return to the winners. Life's cruel and judges have to be ruthless.

The poetry comp scene

There are thousands of poetry competitions around, and the largest ones attract thousands of entries. A small comp with a modest first prize can still draw several hundred poems. In fact, some people think that the huge number of poetry comps will be self defeating; that the bubble will burst and they will fade from the writing scene. The reverse seems to be true. The more competitions that run, the more people get to hear about them, and there is never any shortage of writers pitting their skills against their fellow poets.

As I see it, there are four important factors helping to secure the future of the poetry comp:

● The prospect of finding fame as the result of a win is particularly attractive to poets. Their traditional route to wider acceptance and recognition is longer, slower and more tortuous than the one prose writers usually follow. Competition success brings instant recognition.

● Competition success also brings instant rewards in terms of cash. Of course, poets are supposed to be starving in garrets and, unfortunately, some editors take that too literally. This results in the situation where a short story or article writer can command a good fee for everything he sells, but a poet receives a derisory sum in return for his work. For example, quite a modest prize in a short story competition may match the fee the writer would get if he sold the same story to a women's magazine. If the same sum of money were a prize in a poetry comp, it could represent at least a hundred times the amount the poet would be paid for publication in a small press magazine.

116

● Outlets for the publication of poetry are considerably less well publicised than prose outlets. I said before that it took me a long time to find out about poetry competitions. It had taken me considerably longer to discover small press magazines. Short stories appear in women's magazines on sale in every newsagent's in the country. Poems appear in literary magazines with a tiny circulation, no advertising, and usually available by mail order only. So poets can remain in ignorance of the small press scene for years, even though they are dying to test their talents. Then they might stumble on information about a comp in the local reference library, for example, and recognise this as a possible testing ground. They are delighted to find a showcase for their work, and rush to enter – and then immediately start looking around for information about the next comp. It's easy to see why some poets concentrate much more on competitions than on aiming for publication, which again helps to swell the interest in comps and secure their future.

● Even in the case of writers who seek publication rather than competition success, the winners' anthology may be seen as their best chance. An anthology may cream the top 5%-10% of entries for inclusion. On the other hand, many small press magazines only publish around 1% of the poems they receive. So statistically the publication seekers who use comps as a way in have a greater chance of fame than those who submit to magazines.

I know from long experience that it's unrealistic to expect to win a prize every time you enter a poetry comp, but you can gain a good measure of success if you aim to be in the top 10% of entries, and with luck it's only a matter of time before the awards roll in.

But before you sit down to dash off the perfect competition poem, here are a few points about poetry comps which will help to give you an edge.

The pre-planning stage

Cherish ideas

The quality of poetry competition winners is phenomenally high. I often come away from an adjudication promising myself I'll never write again, because the winners clearly have so much more talent than I do; that my time would be better spent on some useful activity like straightening paperclips.

But as I'm not just a competition junkie but also a poetry junkie, sooner or later withdrawal prompts me to have another bash. And I swear I'll try that bit harder in order to attain the standard of the last comp I judged.

Of course, it's essential to begin with a brilliant subject, but that is not enough to make your poem a winner. However marvellous the original idea, it must be explored and exploited until it develops into a brilliant poem. The poem's construction must be not merely good, but flawless. I'll come back to this point later in the chapter.

Whatever the circumstances prompting you to write, I think you should constantly be on the lookout for a poem with competition potential. (Naturally, this presupposes that you are entering an open comp with no restrictions on form or subject matter.) However much you want to enter any comp, you can't always write an amazing poem to order. You can sit and sweat over your notebook for four hours and still produce nothing more than an elaborate doodle of your monogram. For occasions like these, you really need something to draw on. Similarly, there may be other occasions when you are not even thinking about writing a poem and a good idea pops into your mind.

These ideas are a very special gift, and you don't get them every day. If I get three or four a year I think I'm lucky. So if an inspired idea like this does arrive, it's important to be alert to its potential and nurture it with care. Drop everything to scribble it down. Be ruthless. Abandon the board meeting, the housework or feeding the baby. Those things will all be around later. The idea will drift off into the ether if you don't harness it to paper.

As I said, you can't predict the regularity with which these gems appear. You simply have to be thankful when they do.

But if you keep them together in a file, and add them to all the other poems that excited you while you were writing them and impressed you when you revised them, you will soon build up a portfolio of your best material. The cream may reach the quality demanded for a competition win. While you dip into the file to find poems to submit to comps, keep adding to the portfolio. Consider every poem you produce as honestly as you can. Each time a truly exciting new idea comes along and you manage to produce something fantastic, put it in the file. (Don't be modest about it – acknowledge your skill and be thankful.)

Above all, make sure that you never send your competition quality material away for publication until it has pulled its weight and won you a prize. You're squandering a wonderful opportunity if you send your precious poem to a magazine that "pays" you with a free copy. Remember, few competitions will accept published work. However, a competition winner that has not appeared in a winners' anthology can always find a home in a small press magazine.

Read, read, read

I firmly believe that the best way to keep yourself alert to the quality of your writing is to absorb plenty of poetry. Read voraciously – cover the classics but concentrate mainly on contemporary poems. Read anthologies of winning pieces, single author collections, small press magazines and themed anthologies. Listen to broadcast poetry on local and national radio stations. Attend poetry readings and watch audience reaction. A poem that goes down well at a reading is not necessarily a competition winner, but the fact that it has found popularity should make you think about the standard of its content and construction and ask yourself whether your work would measure up to it.

Some writers don't like to read the poetry of others, and I think they're sadly mistaken. This absorbing of the poetry of other people is not so that you can copy their ideas or offer pale imitations of their work. It's a way of keeping your mind tuned in to the poetry wavelength and keeping the inner radar honed and ready to accept ideas from any source – from your dreams, imagination, fantasies, experiences or observations of the world and the people around you.

And, yes, if you are inspired by somebody else's poem, so what? You're not going to rip it off – in fact, if you're even thinking of doing so, have another look at Iain's cautionary tale in Chapter Seven – you are simply following the legitimate device of triggering your own thought processes through a stimulus.

While you're reading other poems, you should always be on the lookout for original treatments of ideas. You might find that a poem is narrated from an unexpected viewpoint, with a minor character or even an inanimate object telling the story. Perhaps the originality lies in the fact that two or more threads of experience are woven together in the poem. A profound event may be described alongside a more trivial happening, or with the backcloth of a certain location, or with references to fears, memories or emotions. Maybe the content of the poem has been explored in an unexpected way.

Take it all to pieces

You should be reading as a writer, not just for the pleasure of absorbing the text. Keep asking yourself why the poet chose to start at that point, how he developed a logical route through the poem, or how he wove the various strands together to produce a complex, composite picture. Put yourself into his mind and place his blank page before you; then work out for yourself how he filled it.

When you have decided how the poet came up with his good idea and a fresh treatment, when you have also analysed the thought processes that fuelled its conception and the way he brought it to life on the page, then you can apply the same thought processes to your own work. It doesn't matter whether you were able to guess correctly how the other writer managed to find an original approach. As long as the technique you ascribed to him can work for you, the exercise has been useful.

You don't have to restrict yourself to a single reading and analysis of the poem, and then produce a single poem yourself. Fuel your curiosity by asking constantly: *What if he'd started at a different point in the story?* or *How effective would it have been if he'd used free verse instead of rhyme?* Discover the answers by experimenting with more pieces of writing. I often try an idea in a number of different forms and using different angles before I decide which is the most effective. The bonus of doing this is that you can end up with unexpected additional poems under your belt.

By whatever route you channel your ideas into a poem, and whichever writer's stimulus prompts you to produce poems for your comps file, remember that the most telling and resonant voice is your own. You must write with sincerity, with your own integrity. You can't fake it – you must be genuinely involved in the poem you're writing, or you will never convince the judge that you wrote with that essential element: passion.

I believe there are two particular requirements for any poem you write for your competitions portfolio. The poem must be significant, and it must be special.

Have a message
There should always be a reason for writing any poem – or else why write it? A competition poem needs to have a special level of significance. It should open chambers in the mind of the reader, and occupy an important space there. It should insist its message to such an extent that it won't let the reader go. Several years on, and tens of thousands of manuscripts later, I can remember the message in poems I've judged in the past. These had enough significance to insinuate themselves into my thought patterns, almost to make themselves organic and to become a part of me. That sounds melodramatic, but it's true. A poem or, indeed, any piece of writing which can do that has to be a winner.

You can't inject significance into a poem. It burgeons while the piece is being written, defies attempts at definition, and simply exists as an added dimension to the best writing.

To be sure that your poem is significant, remember the advice about writing with integrity and with passion. It won't guarantee that the result is significant, but it will help.

The specialness has as much to do with the respect you have for your own poem as anything else. A special poem is one that has been crafted with care and concern, one that communicates its message to the reader with panache, and makes him feel a frisson of excitement – that tingle down the spine occasioned by the sheer magic of the words. It's up to you to inject the magic – the reader's imagination will do the rest.

Picking a subject

The single most important factor in determining a winning poem is the choice of subject matter. A poem that makes me think, or question, or see things from a different point of view is already part way towards winning a prize.

Without doubt, the subject of the poem should be arresting and exciting. It should not be banal or hackneyed and it should speak out with clarity.

I've already talked about the need for originality in poetry, but it's hard to know which ideas are original and which are not. In fact, even if you follow the advice to read plenty of poetry, you may not realise just how many poems on certain subjects land on the judge's desk. These are the poems that don't make it to the winners' anthology, so unless you can attend the adjudication and prizegiving, or alternatively hover close to the judge's dustbin and examine the rejects, you are unlikely to know what didn't find favour.

This list of "turn off" subjects will give you some insight into the ideas least likely to wow the judge.

Death

It can be very therapeutic to write about death. It is one of the certainties in life, and a contemplation of our own mortality faces every one of us. Any philosophical question lends itself to consideration in the form of poetry, and so the great mystery of anticipating his own death is a sure-fire subject for the poet. No matter how you approach the subject, however, somebody has been there before. There are no answers in this topic – only questions. And people have been asking these questions since the beginning of time, and writing poems about their seeking after truth. Because there are no answers, poems about death are necessarily vague and abstract. Prize winning poems need to be specific and concrete.

Writing about witnessing death is equally common. If you have ever been present at a death, you will know what an astounding experience it is. Again, it's the natural recourse of the poet to chronicle the experience. Unlike the contemplation of death, seeing somebody die is a focussed occurrence, so it is possible to write a detailed, concrete poem about it; but again, it's extremely difficult to be original.

Bereavement

This is the logical follow-on to poems about death, and it can be enormously helpful to the poet, on a personal level, to write about loss. But here, also, we are dealing with a common experience, and one about which poets have been writing for generations. The universality of bereavement makes it hard to find anything new to say on the subject; so you must work very hard to discover an angle that hasn't yet been covered.

A large entry of bereavement poems is found in every open competition. Although they are certainly therapeutic to write, they quickly become tedious to read; and that statement is intended to be realistic, not callous.

By all means dedicate a poem to the memory of your child, parent, partner, or favourite animal and describe your feelings after their death; but see this as an exercise in the grieving process, not as a poem to be entered in a competition.

The beauty of nature

Yes, nature is beautiful, and yes, we should celebrate the fact. But a poetry competition is not the best forum for a declaration of that sort. The topic has become hackneyed. Of course, an original treatment could resolve that problem. But the trouble is, it's very difficult to write originally and in depth about the beauty of nature, especially if you are trying to produce a powerful, specific poem.

The strongest poems are multi-layered, yielding more and more of their essence to the reader every time he looks at them. It is hard to inject additional layers into an appreciation-of-beauty poem, the best of which tend to offer a surface read rather than something more.

If you are determined to write on this theme, try to avoid the amazing sunset and the afternoon stroll through the woods or on the beach. These are the areas that are the most fertile and inspiring, and therefore those that have been done to death.

The cruelty of nature

Although this offers a bit more bite (no pun intended) it has been treated too many times to give much scope. A description of an alligator catching its prey, or the elderly, sick elephant wandering off to die, or the purring, tame pussycat who turns into a ravening monster of a mouse scarer between the hours of dusk and dawn is difficult to suffuse with fresh ideas.

Even if you can offer a clever link, comparing the natural element with something entirely different, you are unlikely to find a convincing comparison that has not been used repeatedly before. You might, for example, list the nocturnal habits of the mouse scarer and compare them with a holiday in Ibiza. Each area provides its own list of images, its own vocabulary and its own series of resonances. When you put them together the combination will offer you a more original poem than either set of material could on its own. But the fact that the prowling cat is so very familiar makes it unlikely that the combined content could be sufficiently fresh and different. (The idea of combining elements in a poem works best when neither strand is too familiar.)

Kids and animals

It's a sad fact, but your sweet children or cute pets are only sweet or cute to you. The rest of the world is not interested in your eulogies about them, and that includes most competition judges. In fact, anything cloying about a child is likely to make even the most sensitive judge grit his teeth and reach for the next manuscript.

The cuteness of your pet diminishes in direct proportion to the number of lines it takes to describe the phenomenon. Holding and stroking a hamster, kitten or iguana may be a delightful activity. Looking at a photo of it is pleasant. Reading ad nauseam about its exploits is mind-numbingly dull.

Cupid's arrow

A "good to be in love" poem has the same problems as the bereavement poem. It's almost too familiar to communicate. The majority of people know the feeling, and even those who can articulate the emotion, bringing the sensation vividly to life, can seldom find anything new to add.

A poem about being in love is usually about a living person, and there is something uncomfortably private about a piece dedicated to another human being. It excludes the reader.

Unrequited love suffers from the same problem. There is something slightly voyeuristic about reading a poem expressing love – and incredibly voyeuristic about reading a poem which expresses love for somebody who is unmoved by the affection. This makes the poem discomforting to read – rather as though you were reading a private letter in the boss's office when he'd gone out to lunch, and he suddenly came back. The judge feels as uncomfortable as everyone else in this situation.

A sea of blue

Contemplating the vastness of the ocean is better done than talked about. The thrill of the elements, especially of earth and water, inspires enormous numbers of poems, and along with love poems, element poetry rivals work about death as the most popular topic with new writers still learning their craft. So the judge approaches the entry anticipating a poor piece of writing.

I'm aware that saying things like this makes me sound biased against poems by inexperienced writers, but nothing could be further from the truth. In fact, most of my working life involves helping new writers, and nothing gives me greater pleasure than to share the joy of a writer's first acceptance or, even more exciting, his first competition win. Unfortunately, experience of adjudication has taught me that certain themes tend to be embraced by poets whose work is steeped in elementary flaws. Reluctantly, I have to admit that they're the traps most writers fall into when they are new to the game.

If you are a new writer, please don't be deterred from entering competitions. Just be sure to iron out the flaws before you post your entries.

Picture painting

A "snapshot" poem, painting a word picture of a person, event or place may be appealing but it seldom has any depth. Usually it offers little but a description, failing to explore any themes, develop any resonances, pose any telling questions or inviting us to look for any extra meaning or significance. It is merely a poetic photograph. This can offer a very pleasing poem, but it's unlikely to be strong enough to win a prize.

Birth

In the nature of things, people write poems about those aspects of life that are so vast you can scarcely contemplate them. We've already looked at death and love, but of course this includes the business of giving birth. If the things your child does and says hold endless fascination for you, the act of bringing him into the world is something you'll probably want to shout about from the rooftops, often in stomach churning detail. Male poets tend to be the most enthusiastic and the most graphic describers of the process. Maybe women are keen to forget about the experience, but some men will confide information a woman would blush to tell her obstetrician.

The last place to send such a poem is to a competition – unless (going back to that familiar proviso) you have something stunning and original to say.

Depression

When life gets you down poetry may soothe and comfort you, and giving vent to your feelings can be very satisfying. When you are living with somebody who is depressed, you may desperately need a chance to release your pent-up reactions. But poems about depression rarely have anything to commend them to the judge. By all means write poems about feeling down, and hopefully you will make yourself feel a little better in the process, but don't share them in a competition.

The same holds true of absolute despair, or a sense of complete hopelessness. I can't stress too strongly the cathartic effects of "writing out" the trauma in poetry, but the resulting outpourings may be a long way from a prizewinning poem.

Celebs

Members of the Royal Family or other celebrities seldom make good choices as subjects for poetry. We all have views – accurate or not – about individuals in the news, but expressing them is rarely enough to produce a poem. And it's possible that you can become so wrapped up in your personal feelings about these celebrities that you stop concentrating on the quality of your writing and become totally absorbed with the subject, to the exclusion of style and technique.

And remember – fame is fickle. Great politicians, church leaders, and top writers, artists, musicians and actors are destined to live on in the public consciousness, but a lot of celebrities have built-in obsolescence. Write today about a rising pop star or sports hero, and by the time the prize-winners' anthology is published it could be that half the readership won't recognise the name.

If you are determined to write about famous people, make sure you can write about them in an interesting, new way. A re-hash of a magazine feature, physical description, or the narration of exploits that are already common knowledge will not inspire the judge.

Ecology

However strong your social conscience, and however important you consider this subject, it's difficult to write a poem about it without becoming didactic – a style to be avoided at all costs if you are writing for a competition. The old style of didactic poetry, with its hectoring or preachy tone, lost favour years ago, and is unconvincing today.

If I have any latent tendencies towards anarchy, they are most likely to manifest themselves when I'm being lectured by a poet. And the only way I can retaliate is by losing interest in the poem. (That might sound like a deliberate act, but it isn't. If the poem is didactic, there's no interest anyway.)

Wars and catastrophes

The latest disaster is unlikely to yield a winning poem. I am sorry if this sounds brutal, and it is not intended to trivialise anyone's misfortune, but natural catastrophes or horrendous crimes can be so vast in their awfulness that it becomes near impossible either to write with focus and precision or to analyse the poem you write about them.

It's far more effective to write retrospectively about such topics – especially wars. What you lose in spontaneity is often recouped a hundredfold by the more balanced, reasoned ideas and images you can draw after a period of time has elapsed to distance you from the experience.

Remember, too, that the disaster prompting you to write is giving lots of other poets the same signal. I was once judging a comp just after the appalling murder of a child. I read a poem on the subject, and was very moved by it, even weeping aloud as I read. But eight or ten manuscripts further on, the same subject occurred again, and it cropped up with monotonous regularity until I'd read about a dozen treatments. It's an awful thing to admit, but by the time I'd analysed a dozen poems on that subject, my natural feelings of distress had been eroded completely, and I had to struggle to be sufficiently objective to give those particular poems a fair chance.

Expressions of faith

Religious poems, usually with the theme "Isn't God good?" or maybe "Isn't God unkind?" should be avoided. Once again, this is material that has been covered many times in the past, and whether the content consists of a broad smile, a loud wail or a whispered carol, it's extraordinarily difficult to inject a fresh voice into the poem.

If you are determined to submit religious material, it may be especially useful to check up on the judge to see if you can find out whether he has connections with any faith. (You can often make an educated guess about this after looking at his work.) There's something about the subject of religion that can put blinkers on the fairest of judges. Remember that a judge will always try to adjudicate on merit – on the quality of writing and the ability to communicate a message – even if he does not agree with the message itself. But you're giving him a difficult challenge if you're trying to convince him on a point where your opinions are diametrically opposed to his.

The same situation is true with politics. In theory, an extreme left-wing judge will be scrupulously fair to an overtly right-wing poem. But if the comp results in a number of entries of similar merit rising to the top of the pile, subjective reaction plays a part, and the writer whose ideologies are at odds with those of the judge may be disadvantaged.

All this is not to say that you should make a point of avoiding writing on controversial themes, nor should you avoid submitting the results to competitions. But be aware of the fact that you might just be prejudicing your chances if the work you submit is argumentatively controversial.

Disgusting material

The final category is things that set out to shock or repel. Anything that is designed to appal or disgust and has been included simply in order to create that effect is much more likely to disappoint. Probably the judge has seen it, written it and matured beyond it years ago.

This doesn't mean that you should "soften up" a poem whose dynamics demand something gritty or offensive. But it makes sense to ensure that the points in question really are essential. Look beyond the immediate shock potential to consider carefully what the poem as a whole is communicating. If the answer is "not a lot" then it's time to reject the poem and move on. (Why not have another look at Chapter Five if you're unhappy about doing this!) If, however, you conclude that the shocking content is vital, leave it in and submit the poem.

As I said earlier in the chapter, this list is not a definitive guide to subjects that don't stand a chance in a poetry comp. It is merely a range of ideas that may not have as much potential in the competition world as you might have thought – although if a poem on any of these themes reaches an appropriate level of competence it could well be acceptable for publication.

Never forget that any idea which you can work into a wonderful, original treatment is worth pursuing – no matter how many times it has been written about in the past.

Poetry checkpoints

Sorry if this next bit seems to be too basic for you ... but please have a look at the list and think about it carefully. I have to reject far too many competition poems because their writers didn't think about these things.

However exciting your choice of subject, you won't win unless you have crafted the poem to perfection. An inspired outpouring is not a poem, but a series of preliminary notes or a rough first draft. Much careful moulding is required to build a poetic structure through which you can communicate your message.

Never underestimate the importance of getting the details right. It's in the attention to detail where a poem wins or loses a competition. You may find it a good idea to pay particular attention to these points:

Form

If the comp is for poems in a set form, make sure you know how to write this. Read up on it if you're in the slightest doubt. I once judged a comp for sonnets in which almost 20% of the entries were not written in iambic pentameter. This meant they eliminated themselves immediately, and made the task of adjudication a lot easier. Those people would have been better off spending their money on a book explaining poetry forms and techniques rather than entry fees. If so, they would have seen a note of the metrical requirement.

Set forms may require a particular number of lines, pattern of rhyming, use of repetition, specific line length and metre. Get them wrong and your poem will not merit a second glance.

If a set form comp is open regarding subject matter, check that your intended subject is compatible with that form. It would be difficult to write a villanelle that narrated a lengthy story, or a ten stanza ballad comprising the lyrical description of a flower. Use the dynamics of the form to complement your material. A tautly controlled, powerful subject can be conveyed through the repetitions of a pantoum. A lengthier, insistent piece might sit more comfortably in a sestina. A lyrical, flowing idea works well in a terza rima. Remember, if any of the forms mentioned in this paragraph is unfamiliar to you, buy a book that explains them (you can always enrol on the Writers Bureau *Art of Writing Poetry* course) or just don't enter a set form poetry contest.

If the competition is open as regards form, you have plenty of flexibility, but remember that a free verse poem is not necessarily an easy option. Although it doesn't adhere to the strict rules of the set forms, it brings its own problems. The line and stanza structuring must work well, and the poem must be the appropriate length to convey your message. Your use of vocabulary and phrasing must be poetic enough to convince the judge that he is reading a poem, not just a prose passage chopped up and printed on separate lines.

Rhyme

If your poem uses full rhymes, make sure that meaning and syntax are never compromised for the sake of rhyme. One of the reasons so many competitions are won by free verse poems nowadays is that rhymed poetry is full of traps of meaning and word order. If the prize can be awarded to a rhymed poem with a flaw of technique or to an unflawed free verse poem, the free verse option will win every time.

Having said this, if all other features are equally good, the rhymed poem may have the edge because of the skills required to get the rhyming right. I love well rhymed poetry, and would prefer to be able to award prizes to poems in rhyming patterns, but because so few attain an appropriate standard, nearly all the winners I select in open competition are written in free verse.

Be willing to spend time playing about with the lines, to find the perfect balance between your intentions for the poem and the limitations of the choice of rhyming words.

Be prepared to change the original word to find a rhyming pair. For example, if you are trying to rhyme a word meaning "unsuccessful" with "beer" then you may struggle. But change "beer" to "ale" and "fail" fits neatly into the next line.

As a general rule, longer lines are easier to rhyme than short ones. The extra syllables you have to play with give you the opportunity to manipulate the wording of the poem without compromising syntax. Also, alternate rhyming lines are easier to work then adjacent ones.

If your rhymed poem demands repetition, remember that any alteration to the wording of the repeated line may weaken the poem. Tiny, subtle variants can give a pleasing tone. Too many make the work appear inept.

Imagery

Conveying the pictures from yourself to the reader occurs through the use of concrete imagery, so that anything the poet is able to perceive through his senses is conjured in the mind and emotions of the reader. The more "solid" the images are, the more clearly your reader will discern them, and the more vivid the poem will be.

For example, don't talk vaguely about "large" or "huge" or "enormous". Paint a picture by using a more descriptive word such as "elephantine" or draw a comparison or use a metaphor to show exactly how big something is.

Good use of imagery adds to the quality of the individual voice speaking out. This individuality of tone will remain in the judge's mind, giving your poem an advantage in the comp.

If you are trying to use concrete imagery, you may need to look again at the subject of your poem. The more global the scale of your subject, the harder it is to work in concrete terms. It is much easier to be precise about the contents of a teacup than about the contents of the universe.

Vocabulary

The words you use to communicate the message in your poem are a vital element. Every word counts. Its meaning, associated implications, and the sound it makes when spoken must all contribute to the final effect.

This doesn't mean that a poem needs to be crammed with fancy language, which can make it heavy and stodgy. Plenty of winning poems are written in short, plain words. The excitement lies in their combination and resonances. Ask a roomful of poets to name the most effective poem they know, and ten to one somebody will nominate Robert Frost's *Stopping by Woods on a Snowy Evening*. It is atmospheric, evocative, thought-provoking – and the longest word in it is the three-syllabled "promises".

A winning poem will probably not contain archaic words and abbreviations such as "thee" for "you" or "morn" for "morning". If I'm the judge, it will definitely not contain any. It will always use specific rather than abstract words, and avoid anything self-consciously over-poetic, like "sylvan", "myriad" or "diadem". It will avoid repetition (unless it is a refrain or other integral part of the poem's form) and it won't over-use worker words such as "the". It is unlikely to contain any adverbs, but will instead use powerful verbs. There will be no clichés or twee euphemisms. Scatalogical words, profanities and obscenities will only feature if they're absolutely vital to the integrity of the poem.

Metre

In a set form competition, more poems are rejected for clumsy handling of metre than just about anything else. Remember that metre is not just a counting of syllables. The natural pronunciation of the language and logical pattern of emphasis should make sure that stressed and unstressed syllables are presented in the correct order. You can't put any ten syllables into a line and call it iambic pentameter. Consider these two examples:

challenging metrical patterns inspire
if metre makes you think, it can inspire

Both lines consist of ten syllables, but only the second contains five iambic feet, ie five consecutive examples of an unstressed syllable followed by a stressed one. So if the idea expressed in both is to be communicated in a poem requiring blank verse, the first would eliminate the poem while the second would be perfectly acceptable.

Do make sure that you are using the right metre for any set form poem. I find it very disheartening to realise that someone has gone to enormous trouble to write a compelling poem in a beautiful form, but I can't award it a prize because one of the lines has lost or gained a foot, or because a couple of phrases break the metre.

Grammar

Some terrific poems fall down because of problems in their grammatical construction. The grammar of poetry may be more flexible than that of prose, but that does not mean you can ignore it. By all means, use language experimentally and with flair. But unless the dynamics of your poem require that you drop traditional grammar, remember that correct grammar will not prejudice your entry, while incorrect grammar might.

It is tempting to use plenty of present participles in a poem, but this often leads to sentences without main verbs. This has prevented more than a few poems from reaching the shortlist.

Pay particular attention to your use of tenses. Confusion of tense is another reason for entries failing to earn a second reading.

Don't forget punctuation. Some poems, of course, aren't punctuated. This may be the way in which the poet makes a statement about his work – or it may be a question of plain laziness and lack of thought or of deciding to opt out of an occasionally tricky facet of the poem's construction. For me, a good punctuated poem always has the edge over a good unpunctuated one. If you set out to use any punctuation, try to be consistent and apply it throughout the poem. Misplaced apostrophes and commas put at the end of a line that requires a full stop are the most common causes of elimination in this area.

Don't skimp on revision

The single most important factor governing a poem's potential to win is the revision you put into it. It's very easy to be so entranced by the magic of your own poetry that you rush it into the post without a second thought. This is especially the case if the comp deadline is looming and you have to mail it today or forget about entering.

Ideally, your poem should be put away for a spell after it's been completed, and then reconsidered later. At that stage, you can be reasonably objective about it, criticising, refining and re-moulding when the memory of all the hard work of writing has been forgotten. But I know how easy it is to procrastinate, and then have to rush the finishing touches in order to meet a deadline. If you do need the poem in a hurry, a quick run through this checklist will help.

- Does the poem have something to say and is it saying it effectively? Are the ideas fuelling the poem and the treatment of those ideas sufficiently stunning to grab the judge?

- Have you kept to the competition's rules? If a set subject or form is required, have you used it? Is it within the length limits?

- Does the pattern on the page look right? Is a set form the best vehicle for the idea, and if so has it been applied correctly? If free verse was used, is the structure natural, with apt line and stanza breaks?

- Has rhyme been applied harmoniously and consistently throughout? Check that the rhyme doesn't take precedence over meaning. If you've used slant rhyme to reinforce a free verse poem, has it appeared often enough to buttress the poem?

- Has metre (if used) been applied correctly?

- Is every word of the poem the right one for its context, so that each phrase, line and sentence communicates power-fully and with precision?

- Is the right quantity of material included, so that the poem neither overstates nor omits some vital element?

When you have satisfied yourself that the poem works on all these fronts, it is useful to put it away again for a while before repeating the process. A few weeks would be ideal – but if you have to get it into tonight's post, a couple of hours will suffice. Go away and do something completely different so that you get into the right frame of mind to repeat the revision exercise with a fresh eye.

As the final part of the revision process, check up on the finishing touches by looking at the opening and the end of your poem.

Have you chosen the right title? This not only creates a powerful first impression on the judge, but it allows you to offer some extra insight into the poem you've written. Don't just tag on a descriptive word or phrase without thinking about it first. Would you be tempted to read a poem with your chosen title? If you would, it's right. If it doesn't inspire you, it won't inspire anybody else. The judge will, of course, go on to read the poem whatever you've called it, but remember that first impressions colour the way you appreciate the work.

Unless the competition is for a limerick or a haiku, the poem should always be titled. Failing to use a title gives your poem an unfinished feel, which looks slapdash and squanders a precious opportunity to anticipate your writing with a word or phrase of introduction. I've already stated that every poem I receive for adjudication is read and considered carefully – but I can't remember retaining an untitled poem in a competition shortlist.

Avoid over-explaining or giving lengthy footnotes at the end. Essential brief notes are fine, as long as they really are essential. If, for example, the poem demanded the inclusion of a dialect word or phrase, this could be defined in a footnote. But resist the temptation to give the dictionary definitions of unusual words – it's a slight to the judge's intelligence. (He can always look them up for himself if he needs to.) Don't interpret the poem for the judge. If he cannot interpret it without help, it won't stand a chance of winning. Remember that the poem is meant to communicate. If it can't do this without the support of sheaves of information, it's failed.

All these aspects of revision and adding finishing touches may seem like a lot of hard work, but nobody ever said that writing poetry is easy. And writing competition-winning poetry is nothing short of hard labour.

Guaranteeing a place in the shortlist

This is a highly misleading heading, as it's never possible to guarantee your poem a place in the shortlist of any comp. It does not matter how perfect your poem is – to find that treasured shortlist place it has to have an indefinable quality that makes it irresistible. And no matter how carefully you have selected your subject and how thoroughly you have worked on all the technical aspects of the poem, the fact remains that imperfect, irrational human choice comes into the equation. Judges have likes and dislikes the same as everyone else, and so their reading of the entries is bound to be coloured by their personal reactions to your work, however hard they try to be objective.

On average, only 10% of the total entry in a poetry comp merits a second and subsequent readings. In a fiercely fought competition, this may rise to 15%. Maybe one in three of these, or somewhere between 3% and 5% of the original entry, reach the final shortlist from which the actual winners are selected.

Just supposing you have followed my suggestion to market study the judge, and learn as much as you can about him. However much you know of his interests in life and in poetry, you can never be certain that your poem will fit his requirements on any specific occasion.

You might enter a poem about a dog, for example, because you know that the judge is a great dog lover and has given prizes to dozens of poems about dogs in the past. But your poem could end up on his desk the day after his precious dog has died, or when his grandchild has been savaged by a dog, or when somebody has just given him a kitten with which he's become besotted. All of a sudden your doggy poem has lost some of its attraction. Then again, the appointed judge might have had to cry off because of illness, and the substitute might be renowned for his terrible allergies and loathing of anything covered in fur.

I'm not saying all this just to put you off, simply to point out that there is more at work than a clinical assessment of your poem. Entering a poetry comp is always something of a gamble. But here are a few final comments and tips to help you beat the odds.

Word perfect

Always remember, the fact that a poem contains fewer words than a story means that a huge weight of attention is focussed by the reader onto every word. A single inappropriate choice can condemn your poem. So while you are writing and revising, you too need to focus all your attention onto each word and each punctuation mark. I cannot stress enough the importance of making sure that every word is precisely right.

I've been forced to eliminate a lot of poems from lists of prizewinners simply because one word didn't work. To know that somebody has lost a substantial sum of money through failing to spot what was probably a typographical error ("out" for "our" for example) is incredibly frustrating. But if there are half a dozen poems of equal merit and the other five are flawless, that typo will be enough to prevent the writer from winning a prize.

The fact is that the final stage of the adjudication is by far the hardest part. In a case such as the one I've described, where a number of extremely good entries jostle for position, you almost end up holding the manuscripts to the light to see if you can spot something wrong with any of them, and can therefore identify a legitimate reason to exclude it. So fine-tuning to the nth degree is essential.

Read it aloud

Remember that the best poetry works on two levels – as a written piece and when spoken aloud. Many poets read their work out loud as a matter of course during the composition process. It enables them to concentrate on the sounds of the words they are producing, as well as their meaning. It also gives an early warning about problems with rhyme, rhythm and metre.

A lot of poetry judges will read all the shortlisted entries aloud. Some record them, and then play them back to assess them on a spoken level. Doing this can make surprising changes to the final results, by nudging a shortlisted piece into the set of winners because of the pleasing effect of a poem when it's read out. I work a lot with spoken poetry, and find that reading aloud is one of the ways to make my mind up in that dreadful final decision stage I've just described.

When you are preparing a poem for a competition, try speaking it loudly and clearly, as if you were delivering it at a poetry reading. If you stumble over a word or phrase, don't worry; it happens to everyone. But if you read the poem again and stumble at the same point, have another look at it. You might find that there's a problem with that section of the poem, and be able to put it right before submitting your work.

If you can find somebody else who'll read it to you, so much the better. Apart from the fact that you might be able to hear any rough patches in the rhyme or metre, you will notice any areas where the reader doesn't quite make sense of the poem, or the handling of the phrasing is not exactly right. As the writer, you can't easily spot these for yourself, because you know what the poem's all about and so read it accurately.

Don't feel you **must** change your poem just because of a hiccough in the reading – but be aware of the need to check over the lines where you stumbled.

Don't explain

Avoid annoying the judge by explaining the techniques of the construction of your poem. He doesn't want to know, any more than the judge of a flower show needs to know what fertilizer you employed, or a music festival adjudicator needs to know how many hours a day you spend practising scales.

Similarly, don't tell the judge that your entry started life as an exercise at a poetry workshop. Competitors always seem especially eager to point this out. There is nothing wrong with entering a poem that had its genesis in a workshop, of course, but information of this sort is not simply unnecessary but unwelcome. The judge wants to see the poem and nothing but the poem.

Above all, don't send a detailed breakdown of the demands of your set form. I once judged a competition in which one of the entries was a pantoum, and the instructions for writing in this form were typed immediately below the poem. Not only was this insulting, but when the pattern of words used looked rather familiar, I checked them and discovered that the writer had copied a paragraph of explanation word for word from one of my books. It had not even been acknowledged. I came to the conclusion that this was a clumsy attempt at a bribe: *I've bought your book, now give me a prize.* Needless to say, the poem didn't win.

139

Not that again

Another way to irritate a judge is to submit the same poem to him time and again. In Chapter Three we mentioned the fact that judges are looking at many competitions every year, and that a judge often adjudicates the same group's competition on a regular basis. Contrary to the opinion of some competitors, you cannot beat the judge into submission by hurling the same poem at him repeatedly in every competition with which he's involved. Too many people send the same work out not just annually, but every few weeks. Sometimes it even looks like the same tired and dog-eared copy of the ill-fated poem.

Virtually all comp organisers publish the name of the judge on the entry form. Be sure to keep a note of who's judging in your competition log, and then you can avoid wasting his time and your money by sending him a poem he's seen before.

I have sometimes been asked whether I've awarded more than one prize to the same poem in different competitions. I'm pretty sure I've never done this, and I'd prefer not to do it. I love the idea of a new, fresh poem being a prizewinner. That's all very well, however, in a competition with a large entry of excellent poems, but in a smaller competition with a less accomplished entry, I could envisage the need to award a prize to a poem I'd honoured before. But a lot of judges are very reluctant to give another prize to a poem they've placed on a previous winners' list, even if the competition rules state that a previous win does not render a poem ineligible.

I have, of course, given the same poet a number of prizes on different occasions, but as most competitions are judged anonymously, that is inevitable. If you can produce one prizewinning poem, you can generally produce a stack of them.

Don't tart up your entry

Earlier on, Iain and I urged all writers to make their entries look professional, with pristine white paper and neat typing or word processing. Poets more than any other writers seem to succumb to the urge to "pretty up" their manuscript. Fancy papers are tedious rather than appealing, and distract the judge's attention from the really important part – the quality of the writing. Plain fonts are much easier to read than fancy ones. Left justified work is much easier on the eyes than centred poetry.

But there's another factor to concern poets in competitions. For some reason, too many of them feel the need to add bits and pieces to their entry. Little notes explaining how and when they wrote the poems are irrelevant. Snapshots of people and postcards of local scenes serve no useful purpose. The only time when an attachment of this type is required is when the comp rules demand it. For example, the theme might be "paintings", and require entrants to send a postcard depicting the painting that inspired the poem. But if nothing is specified, don't add anything to your entry.

Be daring

As every writer is sending in his most stunning work hoping to win a competition, make sure that your entry is just that little bit better than all the others. One of the ways you can achieve this is by being experimental. Take risks. Go over the top. Allow your poem to shine, to brag, to grab attention with its innovation and strength.

Remember, the main aim of the poem is to be memorable, to insist that the judge retains it through the long elimination processes. If there is something a little offbeat about it, it's more likely to have that elusive quality of memorability.

The only snag with this approach is that not all judges will appreciate the innovative power of your writing. You will have to trust to luck that the one reading your poem was captivated by it. One hint: if there are two or more adjudicators, be a little more cautious than usual. It's almost as if there is some limiting force between two judges that advises against the use of anything that might frighten the horses. And a compromise arrangement invariably favours the more bland, less exciting option.

I once co-judged a poetry competition with an expert on the subject competitors were to write about. He insisted that only the dull, heavy, academic entries should go forward, and he wouldn't even allow me to include my preferred selection of work in the winners' anthology. So anyone who entered a challenging poem thinking it might appeal to me found it was a waste of time, money and effort. Needless to say, I prefer to work alone nowadays.

When you feel you have done all you can to guarantee your place in the shortlist, don't just sit back and wait to see what happens. Pick up your pen and get on with the next poem. The best way to keep your spirits up when you realise that you didn't manage to win, is to know there are still a few pieces in the pipeline. And who knows what the next post might bring ...

9

THE WORLD OF
ARTICLE WRITING COMPS

I'm a great fan of non-fiction competitions. They're tremendous fun and articles offer just as much opportunity as short stories and poetry for a writer to experiment, be quirky and original, and to show off his individuality and skill.

In fact, they're the easiest type of entry to excel with. Even if you're relatively inexperienced and haven't yet developed a dazzling narrative style, you can still produce a well researched and logically constructed article which wins a prize because it covers an intriguing subject no-one has ever tackled before.

So I'm always puzzled that journalism contests seem to be overlooked – or looked down on – by so many competitors. People are always saying to me that non-fiction is routine and dull, a backwater of poor rewards and minor glories that just isn't worth their time or effort. But they couldn't be more wrong!

Article or essay comps are one of the big hidden secrets of the competitions world. Their numbers are growing rapidly, as are the prizes. And they offer new writers an incredible chance to shine.

In this chapter I want to open your eyes to this largely untapped market and offer a few hints on how to turn out a winning article.

Operating in the dark

Okay, I have to admit that at first glance there don't seem to be many journalism comps around. But that's just an illusion. There are plenty out there – you just need to look for them.

Sadly, a mixture of apathy, prejudice and their perceived "unsexy" image means that only a sprinkling make the headlines – and these tend to be travel writing events run by large magazines and national newspapers. But there are dozens of non-fiction contests out there organised by small groups who can't afford to publicise them widely or pay for expensive advertising.

That's why it's important to belong to a writers' circle so that you tap into the grapevine for news of upcoming events.

Often, it's a case of looking away from the beaten track. A huge number of non-fiction contests are run by universities, charities, tourism departments, local government, trade bodies and professional associations. They aren't clued up on how the writing world operates and hence often fail to publicise comps where you and I would easily hear of them.

In fact, unless you work in a specific area or have a job or contacts in a particular profession, it's unlikely you'd ever get to hear about some of them. So always check through any trade papers, parish magazines or union journals that you can lay your hands on. And make a point of regularly popping into your local reference library.

Of course, this is where the Internet comes into its own. A quick search on the web for article writing comps will reveal a staggering amount of contests, on both sides of the Atlantic.

And there are a growing number of newsgroups where other mad-keen compers are itching to share their info with you – especially useful in alerting you to more obscure events and those being run in other parts of the world. We'll talk more about how the Internet can boost your competitions career in Chapter Ten.

In the meantime, trust me on this. They may hide their light under a proverbial bushel, but journalism comps are out there in droves – and are eagerly waiting to hear from you.

The genuine article

There are, of course, any number of different approaches to article writing. No two journalists write in exactly the same way. But in terms of competitions, there are really only four main styles of article that organisers look for and these can be labelled simply as:

- The personal story
- The factual article
- The argumentative essay
- The opinion piece

The personal story

These are "you'll never guess what happened to me" accounts, written in the first person, chronicling the writer's unusual and frequently hilarious experiences as he ventures into unknown territory. He could be going somewhere he's never been before, or trying his hand at new skills. Topics could cover such things as his first date, an adventure holiday to an exotic location, his bumbling DIY efforts, or his disastrous attempts to cook a sumptuous gourmet dinner for his boss.

Alternatively, it could be a "confession" piece where the writer talks about events which have altered the course of his life. Perhaps he has overcome a serious illness or disability or struggled with an addiction. Or less dramatically he may have moved to another country and recounts how he learnt to deal with the demands of a new language and a whole series of strange rituals and customs.

The factual article

These are what most people think of when they hear the term "article" – the sort of in-depth editorial pieces that they read every day in their newspaper or favourite magazines.

A writer has researched a topic and sets out to tell the reader things he doesn't already know about the subject. The aim is to inform, to put over hard information. Unlike the personal story author, the factual writer tends to stay in the background, letting the facts speak for themselves.

Pieces can be either articles (ageless general interest items which can be published at any time) or features (a time-critical backgrounder that offers a fresh slant on a topical issue or current events).

Both are perfectly acceptable as competition entries, but the feature tends to have an edge – not just because it has immediacy and taps into current fashions and trends, but because the writer will have researched it with up-to-the-minute information. I will be talking a bit more about this in a little while.

Also under the "factual article" umbrella are personality pieces – interviews with celebrities, sportsmen, politicians, artists, actors and fascinating local characters. These chatty profiles often make the most entertaining of all articles.

The argumentative essay

Despite what the title might suggest this category of article isn't objectionable or loudly controversial or looking to pick a fight. It merely sets out to argue a case.

The writer aims to sway the reader's opinion – perhaps putting forward a case for lower taxes, or for legalising certain drugs or for banning building on green field sites.

Using relevant facts, statistics and expert opinions to back up what he is saying, he puts forward his arguments, trying at the same time to demolish contrary viewpoints. It's very much like a court hearing with him as an attorney putting evidence before the jury to prove his case.

The opinion piece

These are articles where the writer gets to express his own views and tell the reader how he sees the world – and what he thinks is wrong with it. These are subjective, much in the style of newspaper columns.

The author has much more latitude than he'd get in any other form of article. This is because the reader is alerted to the fact that the writer is "sounding off ". He isn't putting over indisputable facts but is making sometimes quite arbitrary judgements based on his prejudices and dislikes.

He may try to back up what he is saying with hard information – and may quote others who share his viewpoint – but there isn't the same onus on fairness or on providing evidence that an argumentative essay would demand.

What will the judge be looking for?

Chances are the judge will be a journalist so, not unnaturally, he will be looking for writers who have a crisp, no-nonsense, journalistic style. He wants to read work that is concise, well constructed, easy to follow and packed with relevant facts.

That means articles without lyrical affectation and baroque stylistic flourishes, with the facts put over in the most direct way possible. No word pictures, six syllable words or obscure classical references.

He'll expect the competitor to have originality, either being able to find exciting new subjects or introducing a fresh way of looking at an old topic so that it becomes novel and attention grabbing.

In addition, the writer will need: star quality, first-class research, attention to detail, the ability to entertain as well as inform, an eye for the unusual, a firm grasp of the subject, a finger on the pulse of current fashions and reader concerns and an authoritative voice.

Most of all, the judge will be seeking a winning entry which is brimming over with facts, facts, facts!

Don't panic

Sounds a lot, doesn't it? But don't worry. Not every article has to be an earth-shattering piece of journalism, honed to absolute perfection. A cracking good read, packed with information, will usually do the trick – especially in a field of lacklustre or predictable entries.

Of all the qualities you need, freshness is probably the most important. The judge wants to read something unfamiliar and feel he's learning something new and unexplored. If you can do that in an entertaining way, then you're home and dry.

Okay, that's fine for the generalities but how do you put all these ingredients and good intentions together? Let's look at the requirements of each category of article in more detail.

Personal stories

Here the adjudicator will look for someone who is a bit of a raconteur – a writer able to tell a clear, enthralling and engaging tale. It will be someone who can make us feel we are there alongside him as he goes through his adventures or confessions.

We experience the sights, sounds and sensations that he describes. We feel the pain just as much as he does when he hits his thumb with a hammer; we blush just as much at the embarrassing encounter with his future mother-in-law; we feel the same scorching sun beating down as he visits a stunning white-washed Greek village – and we enjoy the taverna wine just as much as he does.

A good personal story writer will elicit an emotional response from his audience – even from a hard-hearted judge. Reading his work will move us – to laughter, tears or a sense of yearning. We'll think: *I wish that were me* or more likely: *I'm glad it wasn't.*

And we'll feel we've shared a few moments with a friend. He was actually there in the room with us, chatting, letting us peek into his world.

The factual article

This stands or falls on its facts – or the lack of them. The judge will be looking for a writer who has done some comprehensive research and understands his subject thoroughly.

A good entry should aim to have one hard fact in every sentence. A 1,000 word piece should have about 20 important facts. And it should always answer all the relevant "FiveW" questions, giving all the Who? Why? Where? When? What? and How? information that the reader will need. At the end of the piece he should have his curiosity satisfied. He should be fully briefed on the subject, not left with any nagging doubts or queries.

Now, it's important to think about how you tackle this research. With many timeless general interest subjects – such as, for instance, the history of manned flight, special issue New Zealand postage stamps or how to make your own mead – it's possible to gather all the information you need from reference books.

But that's going to produce a piece that's dry and worthy, a read without sparkle and pizzazz. Chances are that it will lack any warmth or human element.

You're much more likely to create something that zings if you use people as your source of information and include lively quotes from them.

The judge will be entertained by a mead-making expert telling us all about his passion for the drink and enthusing over the taste and the smell. What won't impress him will be a "personless" piece where you've just regurgitated a few bone-dry brewing facts from an encyclopaedia.

Think about it. The judge is likely to be a journalist. And journalists always gather their facts by interviewing experts and picking their brains. They always include loads of quotes in their pieces – to show the human face of the subject. That's what the judge will expect and demand in your work.

Quotes bring an article to life. That's why a feature piece compiled from interview material is always going to have more chance of a prize than a routine book-based general interest article.

It's only when people actually "talk" that they come to life. A well chosen quote can energise a piece, give it immediacy and impact, bring the reader much closer to the subject and imbue it with a touch of warmth.

A couple of points worth mentioning about quotes. It's not enough just to plump a tape-recorder in front of an interviewee (even an entertaining, funny one) and then just regurgitate the interview straight on to the page. You'll be expected to sift through the material, collating and organising it, selecting only the best, most relevant sections.

Magazines may be happy to print a transcribed "question and answer" session piece, but it is not going to do well in competition. The idea is to show how well you can write, how you marshal the material at your disposal, not how diligently you can copy out the contents of a tape.

Also, it's important to use quotes that show how your interviewee feels – whether he's happy, sad, elated, fearful, excited or optimistic – quotes which let us share those feelings. Bland, factual statements are dull. Aim for lively, attention-grabbing sound bites. Show the personality of the person you're talking to.

Remember, no matter what subject you tackle you are always writing about people – and their emotions!

Argumentative essays

The judge wants to see that the writer can make his case logically and powerfully. He'll be looking to see how well the author uses statistics and other pieces of information to back up his argument. And if the author brings in quotes from others to help prove his point, then the relevance of these and their accuracy must be established beyond question. If you are quoting someone else they must be seen to be an authority – an expert in their chosen field.

It's vital that you know the difference between fact and opinion. Opinions are cheap. Bar-room bores give them out for free. What a judge seeks is well researched facts – information that no-one can dispute – not uninformed assumptions, or layman's guesses or second-hand theories. He certainly does not want you to recycle what you read in some newspaper's leader column.

I'd especially warn against regarding any point you make as a self evident truth. It may be self evident to you but not everyone shares your political, moral, economic or religious beliefs or your vision of the world.

Sometimes an argumentative essay may try to stick to the middle ground, merely examining the arguments on both sides of a debate without coming down heavily on one side or another. But I'd advise against using this format.

This may be fine in the world of academia, but the competition judge will feel it lacks punch, drive and any sense of the writer's commitment and passion. He'll think you're undecided, merely sitting on the fence.

Opinion pieces

Now, many people think that these are the easiest type of article to write. After all, they know what they think. Putting it down on paper shouldn't be that difficult. Right?

Wrong! Putting down what you believe may be quite straightforward, but getting the tone just right is very tricky. It's frighteningly easy to alienate the judge, adopt a hectoring manner or be seen to sneer.

Like good newspaper columnists, effective opinion piece authors know that humour is a key tool in winning over the reader. If you can write with a wry and witty voice, your article will appear reasonable and you'll come across as being warm and likeable. Even if the reader disagrees with what you think, he won't be offended or regard you as being nasty or horrible.

But remove the humour and something terrible happens. Instead of being insightful and wise, you will sound like a pompous know-it-all, tub-thumping and forcing your prejudices on people whether they like it or not.

Lose your cool and it becomes even worse. Before you know it your sense of perspective has gone and you're off on a long, angry, bitter rant. It will seem ugly. You'll seem intolerant, bigoted and objectionable.

Opinion pieces can be huge fun, but try to avoid getting on your high horse too much. Woo the judge, amuse and gently persuade him – don't harangue the poor man!

Funny peculiar

Now, before I move on, I want to talk briefly about humour. I love good humorous writing. Nothing impresses me more than an author who can put over a subject with authority, and make me smile into the bargain. We all adore anyone who can make us laugh.

But writing humorously is a very delicate and tricky skill. So please think about it as a technique that has to be used sparingly, with consideration and restraint.

Too many writers sprinkle lame jokes, laboured puns and tedious asides through their work to try to give it a frothy, funny feel. The end result is usually grating and contrived.

Never try to be a stand-up comedian. Don't use an article merely as an excuse to put over some one-liners or tell jokes. Think of humour merely as the oil to keep the wheels turning. Only use it in tiny drops – not big dollops.

And it shouldn't be an end in itself. It mustn't get in the way of the facts or the message. I believe very strongly that you must have substance in what you're writing about. Beyond the humour, the article must have a serious or insightful point to make. Otherwise, it's no more than a comedy sketch.

Be particularly wary of trying to be funny about a delicate or harrowing subject that doesn't lend itself to levity; or of indulging in sick humour merely to provoke a reaction from the reader. Stay well clear of child abuse, cruelty to animals, bereavement, serious illness, torture, disaster, famine and the like. You will upset and offend readers.

The judge isn't going to pick your piece if he has to defend it to organisers who are scandalised, outraged or sickened.

Top tips

I often see more variety, originality and flair in article entries than I do in the work of people churning out "formula" short stories. And generally, the standard of writing is much higher too.

But even so, many article writers fail to get the most out of their material and are guilty of repeating the same basic mistakes. So here are a few handy hints for avoiding the worst of the pitfalls and making sure your work stands out.

Think laterally about the theme

Go beyond the obvious. Seek the unusual. If the competition is being sponsored by a bank and the subject is *The history and importance of currency* (Yes, themes can be that dull!) don't just go to an encyclopaedia and then churn out a chronological account of when banknotes and coins were first introduced. Have fun with it. Be creative.

Approach the topic from other angles. What about the weird and wonderful things that people have used in past centuries instead of money ... such as seashells, large rocks, pigs, camels! Why not try imagining what we might use in the future. Will we even need currency?

Go for humour. Describe some of the strange people and objects that have been printed on banknotes around the world.

Then there are the unusual facts about currency people might not know – during the early 1930s roaring inflation in Germany meant prices were so high that people needed to transport cash around in wheelbarrows. Or that milled edges were introduced to coins centuries ago to stop people cutting them in half or tampering with them.

What have been the biggest robberies of banknotes? How are they forged and what do the authorities do to stop people faking currency? How long do banknotes last? How much does it cost to print them? What happens to old banknotes ...

There's no end to the list of fresh and stimulating ideas you can bring to this boring theme. All that's needed is some imagination. That's what the judge will be looking for.

Shun obvious topics

If the competition has no set theme, and you're free to choose your own subject, still make sure you steer clear of hackneyed topics. That means avoiding such things as:

- The country's most haunted house
- The origins of wedding customs
- Humorous accounts of canal holidays
- History pieces on past Kings and Queens or backgrounders on members of the current Royal Family
- Halloween pieces which look back at pagan rituals and witch trials
- The history of horror films
- Humorous accounts of learning to drive
- Things to do to keep kids entertained during the school holidays
- The origins of Christmas customs

A useful rule of thumb is to think that if it's a subject that crops up regularly in magazines then it's not unusual enough to interest a competition judge.

Also don't produce pieces which look at headline grabbing scares or social issues that are currently in vogue (unless you have a brilliantly original and unheard of angle). So avoid such things as:

- The effects of global warming and climate change
- The loss of the rainforests
- The corrosive effect of television or the Internet
- Yob culture and the loss of manners
- The break-up of family life
- Food and health scares

- The public transport debate
- The dangers of cloning and genetic manipulation

Duck obvious dates and anniversary tie-ins

Conventional wisdom – and most creative writing tutors – tell you that it is easier to sell your article if it has a tie-in to a specific date or holiday. That's why writers regularly churn out thousands of pieces about Christmas, St Valentine's Day and Easter.

That may be true for magazines but it certainly is not a winning formula for competitions. Unless the organisers have specifically requested articles which have a festive theme or which illustrate the true meaning of a date like Independence Day, avoid hanging your material on these routine, yawn-inducing seasonal "pegs".

The judge wants to think you wrote a piece especially for the competition and are not just submitting it because you missed the deadline for your favourite colour supplement.

The same is true for the more predictable anniversaries. Try to avoid them.

When the 30th anniversary of man landing on the moon approached, dozens of eager competitors all produced entries commemorating this space-faring milestone. They were all good reads, but sadly because all the writers covered basically the same ground they cancelled each other out.

So forget those anniversaries which shout out at you – and everyone else! Go for more obscure ones. Is it, for example, the anniversary of the invention of the safety pin? Or 50 years since traffic lights or launderettes first appeared? Or the anniversary of the use of the first credit card? Little-known anniversaries will amuse and intrigue the adjudicator.

Don't pick a topic that relies heavily on illustrations

It's your writing that the judge wants to see, not your graphic artistry or your amazing skill with a camera. A piece must survive solely on the strength of its words, it must be capable of standing alone as a passage of text.

So a DIY article on how to build your own summerhouse just isn't going to work if it relies on accompanying diagrams or a blueprint.

A piece which talks at great length about decorating techniques won't qualify if it depends on copious photos of paint effects, wallpaper patterns and crackle glazes.

Think before you start. Are your descriptive powers up to capturing the sheer majesty and awe-inspiring rawness of the Grand Canyon? Can you make the reader feel its incredible size, desolation and scale?

If you're describing the career and work of a major sculptor, can you convey the intricacy and cleverness of his work without showing the reader examples of his craft? Especially if his approach is innovative and abstract?

If you're going to struggle to bring a subject to life without pictures, then it's not a suitable topic for a competition article.

Think small

The secret of writing a good article is accepting that most subjects are too wide ranging, too complex, to cover fully in 2,000 words or less.

There's no way, for instance, that you could tackle a huge subject such as World War II or the history of the American Presidency in an article. You'd have barely scratched the surface before you reached your word limit.

So you have to take just one small aspect of the subject and look at it in depth.

Thinking about the two examples above, it would be ideal to write about smaller topics such as the U-boat campaign against the North Atlantic convoys or those US presidents who died in office. Both these subjects would fit snugly into a short feature piece. You would have the space to do justice to each, without skimping on information or rushing over facts.

So always ask yourself: *Am I being too ambitious in what I'm trying to cover? Am I trying to cover too much ground?*

If so, make your subject simpler, shorter and more tightly targeted. Don't allow yourself to become lost in a snowstorm of facts and possible angles.

Stay focussed

Having selected your subject, don't stray off the point or go off at a tangent. Stick rigidly to the path. Be ruthless. Don't allow anything to distract you from the course of the story you are telling.

While researching your piece you may find out lots of fascinating information about how many ships have been lost in the Atlantic over the centuries. You may find out interesting snippets about modern nuclear submarines.

Great. Keep these precious nuggets for future projects but **don't** include them in this one. They aren't relevant. They have nothing to do with World War II.

I see writers fall into this trap all the time. They start off writing about a grand city museum or art gallery and then wander off to describe other amazing old buildings in the same street or talk about a benefactor who donated many of the exhibits and end up writing his life story.

Try to stay on target. Rambling, disorganised pieces don't impress. They never win.

Avoid "names-and-dates" history pieces

History is a fertile source of material for the article writer. The past is a fascinating world of quaint customs, odd ideas and even stranger behaviour.

It's a hugely rich vein of true-life stories, a treasure store of tantalising tales of greed, hope, fear, triumph and misery. Every human emotion and condition is there in our history – betrayal, prejudice, nobility, evil, determination, invention, love and injustice, the fight for a better life, the struggle for survival ...

And that's what a judge wants to read about. He wants you to have dipped into the past and pulled out a cracking human narrative. What he won't want to read is a mundane list of names and dates, a dry as dust inventory of years and titles.

Unfortunately, too many competitors seem to think that visiting a stately home and regurgitating its key dates in chronological order is all that's required.

I've lost count of the number of entries I've seen that read like a building's CV. You know the sort of thing:

Built in 1724 by Roger Blaketon, the building was extended thirty years later by his son.

It remained unchanged until 1801, when it was sold to the Littlemore family who renovated the east wing and added a new library.

A new roof was put on in 1843. And so on ...

Who cares? I know I don't. What I want to hear about is the people who lived there. What were they like? What did they get up to? What was it like to live back in those times? How did they live? What did they wear? What did they eat? How did they earn their money? What were their morals?

I want to be enthralled by the stories that the walls of that stately home could tell. I want the gossip, the scandal, the soap opera tales of the people who inhabited the place. I want the past to come alive. I want to imagine myself transported back there.

It takes a lot of research and imagination. And I agree it's hard work and may seem a tad daunting. But no-one hands out prizes for boring lists of dates.

Avoid clichéd travel pieces

It's a sad fact, but nevertheless true, that TV travel shows, jet planes, cheaper long-haul holidays and the accessibility of the Internet have all made the world a much smaller place. And there's so much information on tap these days about the top tourist destinations that most places will be familiar to readers – even if they haven't physically been there.

It becomes a real struggle to come up with somewhere new, challenging and exciting. Name a destination and it's probably already been written about.

This makes it tough to come up with a travel piece that is going to delight a judge or tell him something he doesn't already know.

So you have to abandon any hopes you may secretly have of turning an account of an ordinary package holiday into an easy prize winner. If you're producing the same version of a shopping trip to New York that a hundred thousand other people could have written, then there's just no point.

The only way you'll grab the reader's attention is if your package vacation entailed you traipsing through the desert, catching a steam train across the Tundra or riding camels through bandit country.

Now, don't get me wrong. That doesn't mean that you need to be Indiana Jones to write an engaging travel piece, but it does require you to be a little more clever and more creative in your approach.

If the destination is familiar, you need to find a new angle, a new way of looking at the place. Don't just plump for the obvious. If you want to write about Florida, don't just churn out a predictable piece on the white-knuckle delights of Orlando theme parks. Avoid the well trodden Ernest Hemingway trail to the Keys.

Find something fresh. How about an article outlining all the attractions and locations connected to alligator watching? That should produce a snappy article – sorry about the pun!

If you really must write about Disneyworld and Universal Studios, tackle the subject from the angle of what they have to offer a disabled visitor. Can someone in a wheelchair have as much fun there as anyone else?

And please try to avoid all the cliché descriptions and expressions people feel obliged to use when they put on their travel writers' hats.

You won't win a prize with ... quaint or picturesque villages (especially sleepy ones or those nestling amongst the hillsides) ... cities that never sleep (with or without streets flooded with a sea of neon) ... sun kissed beaches ... buzzing nightlife ... night-clubs heaving with bodies ... majestic mountains ... breathtaking vistas ... azure blue skies ... crystal clear seas ... or any of the other shop-worn examples of predictable purple prose.

Remember, the judge wants originality in your language as much as he does with your choice of destination and your angle.

Don't submit opinion pieces

Unless the competition specifically requests them, opinion pieces aren't usually that welcome. They tend to make judges groan, especially when they're written in a strident, intolerant and dogmatic way. Whenever I have to read this kind of tub-thumping piece I always feel trapped, as though I've been locked in a lift with an angry taxi driver!

Chances are you'll be expressing a view that will be at odds with the beliefs of the judge/the organisers/the sponsors/most other people. If the winning entries are being published as part of the prize, it's likely that a "safe" general-interest article will be chosen. No judge will select an entry that will offend or upset readers.

If you feel passionately about a controversial subject, keep it short and write to the letters page of your local newspaper. Or stand on a soapbox on the street corner!

Competitions are not the place to target if you want to change the world, or put the cat amongst the political pigeons.

End thought

I'm always urging writers to make their articles light, frothy and full of fun. Aim to please. Try to think of yourself as an entertainer not as a school teacher or someone giving a worthy but dull lecture.

You don't have a captive audience. There's nothing forcing the judge to sit down and read your entry all the way through. Make him want to! Fascinate, intrigue, amaze and confound. Make him go "Wow!"

10

COMPETING IN THE INTERNET AGE

Time was – and not so long ago – that you only ever got to hear about a fraction of the competitions you could enter. Unless a contest was mentioned in the major writing magazines, had a poster up in your local library or its organisers had directly contacted your writers' group, you wouldn't be aware it existed. But in this dizzy new electronic age, that's all changed – and how.

In just a few years the success of the Internet has transformed the competitions scene beyond all recognition. If you have a computer, the world is now at your finger tips – a world packed full of prize-winning opportunities.

By "surfing" the Net you can gain access to thousands of exciting contests, all at the click of a mouse. And you can compete on an international stage – pitting your best against writers and poets from other countries, perhaps even from other continents!

And the Internet has opened up an exciting new market for competition fans. A whole generation of e-zines – electronic magazines – have sprung up. These mags exist purely on the Internet and are often run by young, ground-breaking editors. They frequently host competitions for challenging new fiction and poetry, the type of material that would be too cutting-edge and experimental for more traditional competitions.

The possibilities are boundless. There is a mind-boggling number and variety of contests to select. But that's only part of the Internet story. It's a God-send to all writers, particularly those article writing competitors eager to research complex subjects, gain access to foreign information sources and pick the brains of experts. It's also a vital tool to all competitors keen just to swap views and competition news with others.

In this chapter we'll show you how the Net can help you in your writing and research. We'll also tell you how "electronic" competing can speed up your entries, make the whole process cheaper and easier, give you more choice and enable you to wave goodbye forever to that last-minute manic dash to the post box.

Here today, gone tomorrow

A quick word before we plunge on. The Internet is a vibrant, dynamic and constantly changing place, and websites and e-zines can pop up in a burst of enthusiasm and disappear just as rapidly. Nothing stands still for long.

That means that it's impossible for us to promise that every single site we mention in this book will survive long-term. Some will fold, change editorship or direction. All we can offer here is a snapshot – a moment frozen in time.

If a site we recommend has disappeared, please accept our apologies. To counter this we have tried to list several similar websites wherever possible so that if one has gone, the others will still be working.

The moral is to always keep surfing, regularly updating your list of favourites and freshening up your market research. Every time you look you'll find something new and exciting to catch your attention.

What is the Net?

Okay, before we start the hard sell, let's talk about exactly what the world wide web is. After all, not everyone has a computer yet and who knows, what we're about to say about the advantages of being linked up to the web might make you rush to buy one.

Basically, the Internet is a link-up of millions of computers and databases around the world. It's a cross between a gigantic telephone exchange and a vast international library.

You can use it to send information to computers on the other side of the planet. Or you can call up websites – pages of text and pictures – that individuals or companies have set up for others to view and use.

No two people use the web in exactly the same way. You can think of it either as the largest notice-board in the world or as a reference book with an infinite number of pages covering a multitude of topics. You can use it to send and receive e-mails – the electronic equivalent of letters – and can share news and views with others in multi-link-up chat-rooms and newsgroups.

Some people like to think of the Internet as a world of its own – a land with no national or cultural borders – a place that exists in its own cyberspace. It has its own clubs, magazines and meeting places. Membership is open to everyone. All you need is access to a computer – so go and buy one! It's the shape of the future.

A world of opportunity

We've said in Chapter Two that the Internet is a great place to find competitions – especially foreign competitions – but what most writers don't realise is the sheer breath-taking scale of possibilities.

There are more competitions out there than an army of writers could tackle. To prove the point we did a few simple searches on the *Google* search engine. The whole process took less than five minutes.

By entering the words "writing competitions" the computer came up with a list of 117,000 entries. And that's just using one search engine! Think how many more you could find using the many dozens of search engines that exist.

Our search found 41,500 sites listing poetry competitions, 20,000 on essay writing and 27,000 devoted to article writing comps. The number of sites detailing short story contests was a staggering 45,800. And these are being constantly updated and amended.

Now we're not suggesting you attempt to visit all of these sites – or even a fraction of them. But it does show what is out there. You might find it easier and less hassle to visit just a few recommended sites. We've already suggested in Chapter Two that you keep a close eye on www.gsp-online.com and www.writing-world.com but there are other great "shortcut" sites to sample. We'd recommend you try:

www.writerswrite.com
www.writersdigest.com
www.stories.com
www.e-writers.net
www.openingline.co.uk
www.poetryonline.com
http://web.liswa.wa.gov.au/writcomp.html - this site
lists Australian competitions

Whenever you surf and find a new comps site or an e-zine devoted to comps, make a point of adding it to your "favourites" list. You will be surprised at how quickly you can build up a comprehensive data base of likely contests.

Always keep an eye on e-zines. They often run competitions and many display the winning entries of previous events on their websites. This allows you to study what type of stories or poems succeeded.

Do your homework before entering. See if you spot any trends or themes in what the editor has picked. See if you can get inside his mind and work out what he likes.

Horror and science fiction e-zines are a particularly good place to target if you have a lively mind and produce material that is unconventional, cutting edge or more disturbing than mainstream competitions usually favour.

Once again a quick search will provide you with more e-zine sites than anyone could possibly read through – even in a year. Two good sites to point you towards interesting e-zines are www.ezine-universe.com and www.etext.org.

At the touch of a button

Having an endless supply of comps to enter is wonderful, but that's only one facet of the Internet. One of the most satisfying things about the web is the way that it takes the waiting out of competing.

Normally you see a few sketchy details on a contest printed in a magazine and have to send off for the full info, plus an entry form. This can take weeks to arrive, only for you to find out that there's a restriction in the rules which bars you from entering.

On the Internet everything is instant. When you find a competition that appeals you can read the background and rules in full on the screen there and then. If there's an entry form it's usually displayed there for you to print off. So much for waiting for the post to arrive.

Many competitions exist purely in cyberspace. Organisers – usually e-zine editors – ask you to transmit your entry to their e-mail address. There are no postage costs, no wasted paper, no running to the postbox. And most attractively, no limit to when you submit your entry. If you can't sleep and want to send your entry in the middle of the night while you're wearing your pyjamas no-one is going to know – or care!

And there's no need to send work days before the closing date, just to be extra sure it makes it in time. Your electronic entry arrives at its destination anywhere in the world just moments after you hit the button; so you can leave it until the last moment to enter.

And unlike sending paper entries to "real world" comps, you'll probably get a quick confirmation e-mail note to let you know your work has arrived safely. A computer can send hundreds of confirmations without breaking into a sweat – unlike a poor, overworked, human organiser!

Group hugs

It's fast, it's easy, it lets you try new markets and comps on the other side of the world, but one often overlooked attraction of the web is the friendship it offers. No, we're not suggesting that you hug your machine or buy it Christmas presents. What we're talking about is the ability it gives you to make new friends, right across the globe.

Writing can be a lonely business, especially if you are housebound or live in a remote area that has no writers' groups to join. Sometimes it feels like you've got no-one on your side, no-one to chat to or have a moan to when you hit a run of bad luck.

But the computer brings a whole "virtual" community of writers right into your home. It lets you electronically "touch base" with people who are just as dotty about entering comps as you are.

News groups – on-line writers' circles – make it possible for you to converse with like-minded scribes and poets. These are open-to-all public discussion groups. People put on messages which can be simultaneously read by everyone else in the group. The messages are shown as a list, known as a "thread", that displays the original e-mail that kicks off the discussion, the responses to the message, and the responses to the responses!

Group members give advice on comps, offer news on websites of interest to compers and give warnings about scam contests and dodgy anthologies to avoid. Some people even "post" their work to the newsgroup and ask for feedback and criticism – a brave act indeed.

Even if you don't want to get actively involved, you can merely scan the e-mails that people send in and can eavesdrop on the conversations, debates and rows that ensue.

Newsgroups are being launched all the time so it's always worth checking to see what's going on. But a few newsgroups it's worth subscribing to are:

alt.creativewriting
alt.writing
uk.culture.arts.writing
england.writing
misc.writing
sdnet.writing
umn.local-lists.writing

And if you don't fancy any of these – you can always start your own! Outlook Express – the e-mail program supplied free with most computers – offers you a comprehensive list of newsgroups to subscribe to with just a click of the mouse. Most internet service providers (ISPs) have direct links on their home pages to newsgroup lists and if your provider doesn't, you can access newsgroups by going to: www.dejanews.com/usenet.

Search me

If you're an article writer and enter non-fiction competitions you'll probably already regard the Internet as a phenomenally useful research tool. It allows you access to millions of sites, bringing a wealth of knowledge from museums, encyclopaedias, fan clubs, news organisations and universities right into your home.

But something that is often overlooked is how useful this can be for fiction writers. The Net can be invaluable in helping you research those details that give your story's setting, characters and background details real authenticity.

165

Writing a story set in a city on the other side of the world, a city you've never visited? No problem. The Internet can tell you all about it – the shops, the neighbourhoods, the crime rates, the night spots, the main buildings ... even down to what the weather there is like at any given moment.

Writing a sci-fi tale set on a rocket? It's easy to find out what conditions your astronauts will experience. NASA's website at www.nasa.gov is a good starting point. Even if you don't have a scientific background you can find enough technical details to sprinkle through your tale so that readers will think you're a boffin!

Writing a story with a historical setting or using a real figure from the past? It's all there – all you'll ever need to know about what life was like in former eras. Suddenly research that would have taken months can now be carried out in a few hours.

Of course, with so many possibilities to choose from, it's all a bit bewildering, but don't worry. Here are a few useful sites that we think you should bookmark. They'll make surfing the net swifter and easier.

The first of these is *JournalismNet* compiled by Julia Sher, a top Canadian investigative journalist. It quite literally brings the entire globe into your home.

This research tool – described by *News World International* as "one of the most popular and respected journalism sites on the web" – is a one-stop gateway to information sites right across the world.

Whether it's finding out about a company in Africa, crime statistics in Spain, climate details for Switzerland or political news from Holland, *JournalismNet* can immediately transport you to where the info is.

Log on to www.JournalismNet.com and you will find a breathtaking amount of US, British and international facts at your command. Pick the country you're interested in, click on it and the site will whisk you to a special home page for that area.

Once there, you'll be able to track down what you need by connecting to any one of thousands of databases, reference books, libraries, museums, TV and news archives and wire services. You can tap into breaking news in all major radio, TV and press outlets or go through their old tape and cuttings collections. There is even a tool to enable you to translate newspapers written in other languages.

The site provides basic background data on the country of your choice. Other information instantly available covers a bewildering array of subjects from religion, culture, health and legal news to weather, human rights, government, sport and business briefings.

The emphasis is strongly on investigative journalism and the site helps you to track down people as well as facts. So it shows how to find people on the web through genealogy and reunion sites, discussion groups and mailing lists. There are tips on tracking down think tank experts and university dons who have just the knowledge and contacts you need, and hints on finding out someone's e-mail address or phone number – no matter where in the world they live. You can play detective without ever leaving the comfort of your living room.

A bonus is that writers in America, Canada, France and Britain all have their own "dedicated" specialist versions of this amazing site.

The American site is at www.JournalismNet.com/US and the UK site is at www.JournalismNet.co.uk.

Themestream is another top site. It bills itself as "the web enthusiasts' resource" and is a treasure-store of articles on more than 1700 topics covering everything from automobiles to Zinfandel wines.

The site, to which subscription is free, brings together features and information from professional and amateur authors, speciality publishers, experts and enthusiasts. And it brings it all straight to your e-mail box – you don't have to lift a finger.

Tell the site what topics you are interested in and it will automatically compile customised "newsletters" and regularly despatch them to you.

A quick search under the heading of writing brought up articles on a writer who started up at 40, a guide to poetry mags which pay (very useful!), advice on keeping a log if you regularly enter literary competitions, dreams as a source of inspiration for stories and a detailed explanation of how to write an authentic sounding crime scene. It's well worth a visit.

A great tool for making net searches quicker and easier is the oddly named *Dogpile* – at www.dogpile.com. This is more than just a simple search engine, it is a powerful seek and locate service that simultaneously contacts more than a dozen individual search engines and looks through their databases as well as its own. So every time you type in a request, you're not just getting Dogpile searching for you, you're also getting top name search engines like *Yahoo*, *AltaVista*, *Google* and *Lycos* joining in the hunt.

With all that search capacity working for you, tracking down the right web pages becomes a mere doddle.

You can even have an Internet butler working for you! *Ask Jeeves* at www.ask.com is a unique search engine. Instead of just typing in "key" words for the machine to look for – like "writing" or "competition" or "adjudicator" – you actually ask Jeeves complete questions. So you'd ask him, for example: *Where can I find out about article writing competitions?* and he'll come back with links to as many as a hundred sites.

A neat trick. This is one virtual butler who does everything but polish the silver.

Watch out, there's a scam about!

The Internet is ideal for finding contests, researching articles and putting you in touch with other comp-mad writers, but there's one benefit we haven't mentioned yet that makes it advisable to be on the web. This is the arena where many scam competitions and rip-off anthologies are exposed.

If you are operating on your own it's unlikely that you'll have insider knowledge of these organisations which prey on the unwary and the gullible. But those on the Net can name the guilty men – and do!

For example, popular e-zine *Wind Magazine* has gone a long way to helping put dodgy comps under the microscope. It's compiled an online library of cautionary articles, exposing the worst poetry scams and showing how they operate, naming names on which competitions to avoid and chronicling case histories of writers who've been conned and parted from their cash.

Simply go to http://wind.wind.org/literary.scams.htm for the links page to this useful and frightening rogue's gallery of dodgy dealers and their methods. It's guaranteed to shock and put you on your guard.

We've already pointed you towards newsgroups, but one worth noting is alt.writing.scams. This acts as a bulletin board for writers, allowing them to warn each other about dubious comps and awful anthologies. It's not been running for long but it aims to be constantly updated with alerts about any new scam competitions springing up. As well as reading any warnings, you could add your own "watch out" messages by e-mail if you encounter shady dealings.

Incidentally, we shall be looking at the pros and cons of anthologies and what to avoid in the next chapter.

Convinced?

We hope you are. These are just some of the arguments for competitors to look upon the Internet as a useful resource in their prize-seeking campaigns. But it's likely that as more and more writer-interest sites come on line in the future, being on the web will be a crucial factor in getting an edge over your rivals.

So if you aren't already an Internet fan, give it a whirl. It'll open up a whole new world to you. Who knows, you might be about to become a star on another continent!

11

ANTHOLOGIES

We've already mentioned anthologies of prizewinning work a few times, and pointed out that they represent a good way of getting your writing into print. They also serve as a special memento of your success in a competition. The memento is tangible. You can carry the book around with you and have a little peep at it whenever the fancy takes you. You can read it ostentatiously on the train. You can buy extra copies and give them to your friends as birthday presents, or leave a copy lying around on a coffee table and then invite everyone you know in for coffee.

There are, of course, other ways in which your successful writing could see the light of day. Short story, poetry and article competitions are often sponsored by a magazine and so the winning pieces of work may appear in the next issue or a special edition. For example, *Freelance Market News* features competitions on a monthly basis, and the winners are printed.

Poetry prizewinners often appear in literary magazines, but because of the length of a poem, it may be published in different ways. Successful poems are sometimes reproduced on postcards, and sets of cards bearing the winning work are available to buy. They may be framed for display, just as you would frame a photo, or published on posters.

Radio broadcasting is another popular outlet for winners. Both the BBC and commercial stations feature prizewinning stories and poems throughout Britain.

However your material is showcased, you feel a terrific sense of achievement at the recognition it receives. And rightly so – after all, you worked very hard for your success. But nothing quite matches the glow of seeing your competition story or poem printed in an anthology.

In fact, some competitions exist only to provide material for publication in anthologies. There are short story books and literary magazines, for example, that are published regularly and are filled solely with contents submitted as competition entries. Writers send in their work with an entry fee, and the judging takes place in the usual way. Then a collection of stories is published as the new edition of the book/magazine. One or two of the stories are singled out for special praise, and a cash prize.

This is a good way of compiling an anthology. Because you are requesting comp entries, rather than ordinary submissions of material, and therefore charging an entry fee, writers tend to think about their work and send something good. Too many writers are not selective about the material they send to a publication "on spec".

By making it a competition, the publishers are collecting fees to help offset the expenses of publication. The writers who enter will ensure that their work is as good as it can be to justify the investment of the fee they are sending. And the added bonus for the publishers is that they avoid the inrush of thousands of inept pieces of writing which have to be ploughed through.

Some excellent anthologies are published in this way, and offer fascinating reading material; but the system is open to abuse. Have a look at the section of this chapter entitled *An Enormous Caution* and ask yourself a few questions about your target anthology comp before you have any work published in this way. As a general rule, if you have to pay to enter it is more likely to be a genuine comp than a scam or rip-off.

A genuine prizewinning anthology will be crammed with fantastic work, as you will have realised from our descriptions of the difficulty of the adjudication process. So the quality of the content will provide you with a great deal of enjoyment as a reader. But there's an added advantage. If your work is included, you can be sure that you'll find your story or poem nestling alongside material of an equally high calibre.

It's quite important to think about the company your writing keeps. If your poem or story is seen next to excellent work by respected names, it will look far more impressive than if it appears alongside inferior pieces of writing. As the overall standard of writing in a winners' anthology can be so high, publication will bring you the kudos that's compatible with this quality of writing.

When a comp has been organised by a writers' group, the anthology is often launched at the awards ceremony, and writers may have the opportunity to read from it to an admiring audience or to hear the judge or celebrity guest reading successful entries.

If you do get the chance to read your own work, take advantage of it. You can put just the right intonation into your piece. You know which bits should be emphasised and which skimmed over. You know exactly how to build up to the climax in order to have the desired effect on the audience. You can show your work to best advantage. Make sure you do this by rehearsing thoroughly. Yes, we realise that you wrote the story or poem in the first place, and you know it more intimately than the back of your hand. But it may be a while since you looked at it. Although it's a good idea to read your work aloud throughout the creative process, you might not have done this – in fact you may never have heard your piece spoken aloud.

While you are rehearsing, concentrate on speaking slowly, loudly and clearly enough to be heard and understood, but not so slowly that the reading becomes pedantic. When you actually speak your work aloud, take great care with your presentation, and endow every phrase and sentence with just the right tone to enhance the communication of your message.

There is another benefit to reading your own work from the anthology. If you read it well, you are showcasing your abilities in front of a roomful of writers. You might find yourself being invited to give a talk or run a workshop at one of their meetings. If you're a poet, you could get a booking to do a reading. And of course, the more you do, the better known you become. Success feeds on itself to bring you further offers of work – commissions, adjudications and more workshop and speaking engagements.

The presentation of the anthology containing your winning work can take any number of forms. Some are little more than a few photocopied sheets stapled together. Some are neatly bound and attractive, making a useful keepsake. Others are glossy and professional, like a substantial paperback book. Most contain a selection of shortlisted pieces as well as the actual winning entries, so there is plenty to read.

If your work appears in an anthology, you should be given at least one complimentary copy of it. (In fact, you can be very suspicious of the set-up if you are not presented with a copy.)

172

If your own work isn't included, you will have to pay for a copy of the anthology, but consider the purchase a good investment. The winners' anthology often includes a report by the judge, explaining how and/or why he made his final choice. This is invaluable to shed light on what might appear to be a baffling decision (especially if he didn't choose your story for the first prize).

It's worth paying attention to his comments. Whether or not you agree with them, the fact remains that satisfying his requirements gained somebody a prize. So if you can't understand what the judge was driving at when he praised or criticised something, persevere and read it over again.

Always bear in mind the fact that, for the judge, the writing contained in the anthology is the best submitted to the comp. Read through all the contents very carefully, first for enjoyment and then afterwards to make certain you know what made those pieces of writing stand out above all the other entries. If there is a report, make sure you can marry up the comments with the content of the published winning pieces. Even if there is no guidance from the judge to help you understand his choices, it's a useful exercise to try to work out the reasoning for yourself. It will give you a better idea of what is wanted from a competition piece.

If the competition is an annual event, a study of the winners might help you to select an appropriate entry to send in next year. If the same judge is adjudicating, you already have a head start with your knowledge of this year's successful entries. If there's a different judge, you might still have a head start. It's possible that the judge saw only a proportion of the pieces submitted, and that the clearly unsuitable entries were filtered out by a panel of preliminary readers. If this is the case, the same panel will probably be filtering next year, too – or a panel with a penchant for a similar style of writing.

A small caution

Inclusion of your work in a prizewinners' anthology is generally a good thing. It's pleasing for you on a personal level, which is a marvellous boost for the confidence. In an area where there are so many people looking to knock your confidence, this is particularly valuable. Accept the plaudits and the ego boost in the knowledge that the next post could bring a rejection. (We're not trying to dent your ego by saying this – just being realistic.)

Inclusion adds another success to your file or scrapbook, and that too is a cause for celebration. Whether you're a new writer or a highly experienced one, every anthology acceptance adds to your CV and enhances your credibility.

But there are just a few notes of caution worth mentioning. First, be aware that when your work is published, even in a designated winners' anthology, its publication eliminates it from most competitions in the future. We've already talked about the advantages of writing something fresh for comps rather than letting the same piece keep doing the rounds; but sometimes a piece of writing could do a lot more for you than, say, win a minor prize in a small competition. There was a case of a poet some years ago whose poem had received a tiny award in a comp at the local library. As it was still eligible to be submitted, it was also entered for a much larger and more prestigious competition a little while later. It won first prize, a four-figure cheque and instant, large-scale recognition for its writer.

Of course, if your poem or story is a prizewinner, you may feel quite happy to allow the people who've awarded it the prize to publish it in their anthology. That seems only fair. But if your work hasn't won a prize but has still been selected for publication because it was on the shortlist, you're in more of a "Catch 22" situation.

Publication in itself is an acheivement. You should weigh up the advantages of simply getting your work into print. But the piece that reaches the shortlist of one competition has the potential to be a winner in the next. It's good, or it wouldn't have reached anybody's shortlist. We have already looked at the fact that comp entries need to come as close to technical perfection as you can make them. Remember, though, that in the final analysis, subjective opinions count in a writing competition. One judge has clearly recognised the quality of your work. It could be that another judge would see beyond the merely technical accomplishments, and recognise something in it that holds particular appeal for him. He might regard it as exceptional, and give it first prize.

Because any shortlisted piece has the potential to be a winner with a different judge, it could be a waste to allow it to be published. It would be better to wait while it tries its luck in a few more competitions just to see whether it really does have the extra "edge" to make it a prizewinner.

So the question of whether your work should appear in an anthology is just a little more complex than you might have considered at first. But do you have any choice in the matter?

If the rules of the competition stated from the outset that an anthology of shortlisted material would be published and those people who entered were deemed to have accepted the rules when they did so, there's not really much you can do about it. You are honour bound to allow your work to appear. If you have entered under these circumstances, don't fret over the situation. Be pleased to accept the publication, and if you must, gnash your teeth in private and read the small print more carefully next time.

If there is no mention of publication in the rules and you are approached after the adjudication for permission to publish your entry, you will need to think about the question. Under these circumstances, you should feel under no obligation to have your work published unless this is something you want. There should be no embarrassment about requesting that your work be withheld from the anthology. You don't have to give a reason if you don't wish to – simply ask the organisers not to print your writing but to return it to you. The only time they are likely to object is if you are one of the prizewinners. And as we said earlier, you may feel a moral obligation to allow the organisers to publish the entry for which they've forked out a prize.

As you can see, there are arguments for and against the publication of your prizewinning writing. You need to make up your mind about where you stand as regards anthologies, and make your decision about whether or not to enter the comp in the light of your opinions.

If ever your work does appear in an anthology, do ensure that you retain copyright on it. With a prizewinning piece, you have a valuable asset, and while it's fine for the competition organisers to expect the right to publish and/or broadcast on one occasion, further rights should revert to you. Remember, a winning story or poem could be anthologised several times over. A winning article could be reprinted or syndicated. A monologue could be performed on stage, radio or screen. Unless you check that all rights remain with you, you could miss out on some valuable returns from your work and, more importantly, on the control over it. You need to be able to stay in command.

An enormous caution

Despite the caveats mentioned above, the winners' anthology is generally a good thing, and dozens – if not hundreds – of them are produced each year. The work they contain is well selected, they are carefully printed and attractively packaged, and they represent a legitimate, worthwhile publication outlet. But unfortunately there is a large grey area in which some morally questionable publishing practices go on.

Some publishers are in the business of running "anthology competitions", using writers' fascination with comps as a way of attracting a high volume of submissions. Instead of making a selection from the cream of the work submitted, they print all the entries in large anthologies, and expect the writers to buy the books in which their work appears. There's nothing to stop the companies from doing that, and you might think fair enough, it's a legitimate way of conducting business. But before you send any work to them, think about the way the scheme works.

These comps are widely advertised, and more often in general publications rather than in specialist writers' newsletters or magazines. So people who don't know about, or don't subscribe to, literary magazines (or magazines which target writers as their readership) are likely to see the ads. They appear in women's magazines, TV listings magazines, a wide range of daily newspapers etc. The general public, rather than the writing public, will read all the details and enter the competition.

Yes, of course experienced writers will see the ads as well, but the aim of the organisers is to catch the eye of the uninitiated, and persuade them to try their luck. Quite often the comps are free to enter, and in the UK they sometimes offer free postage as well. In fact, with everything being free, the experienced writer begins to hear the warning bells. There may be no such thing as a free lunch, but there are precious few free writing competitions either.

Most of the comps that are run in this way are for poems. Maybe poets are more gullible than other writers, but we prefer to think that the preference for poetry is twofold. First, poems are shorter than stories or articles. People who don't consider themselves to be writers will have a go at a poem, because it represents less time and effort expended. So there are more poems about than there are stories or articles. Also, a surprising number of people write poetry at some time in their life. People who would never call themselves writers will put pen to paper at a time of great emotional upheaval, such as first love or bereavement. When they see information about a free-entry competition for poems, they remember that special poem, get it out, dust it down and send it off.

Secondly, because they're so short, you can get more poems on a page. In fact, some anthology comps set a particularly short line limit to guarantee that at least half a dozen poems will fit on a page. We'll come back to the import of this in a minute.

The organisers of the free competition are in the business of making money. They bait the hook by offering free entry, and then reel you in with flattery. And when you're there and wriggling, they hit you with the request that you purchase an anthology in which your work will appear. This is where they make the money, and they intend to make a lot more of it than they would from small entry fees. It works like this:

1. You see the ad, and submit some work. This may be the most wonderful poem ever written, or it might be utter rubbish. That doesn't matter, because in due course ...

2. You receive a response from the organisers. They tell you your work is fantastic. In fact, they might tell you your poem has reached the shortlist, or that it's in the running

for a major prize. It is definitely going to appear in their anthology. They enclose an order form.

3. You return the order form with your cheque. After all, you want to see your fantastic poem in print, don't you? And there's still the chance that you'll win the big one ...

4. In some cases, you receive another order form. As you've decided to buy yourself a copy, why not get one for your partner/great aunt/milkman? And as a very special offer, there is a tiny reduction in the price. There may be an additional form, asking if you'd like to have some brief biographical details included in the anthology, so that people can put your work into context. You might even be given the opportunity to buy a leather bound edition of the book, with your name on the front in gold. There's only a small sum payable for these services ...

5. Eventually the book arrives. It is extremely attractive, finely printed on good quality paper, and nicely bound. It's a whopper. It's crammed with poems. The pages are A4 size, and there are several hundred pages in the volume. You can scarcely lift it! Your poem is tucked away in a corner on page 476, but that doesn't matter, because you've been told that your poem is fantastic, and certainly good enough to be included in this spectacular book. It turns out that you were not the winner, but you were shortlisted, or even a semi-finalist. Now that you've had an opportunity to see the book, how would you like to buy additional copies for your children/babysitter/bank manager? And as a very special offer, there's another tiny reduction in the price.

6. You read the book, and even if you are the least critical reader on earth, you are appalled by the quality of material that appears beside your own. Why, there's nothing worth reading in any of the other five poems that appear on the same page as yours.

7. A week or two later, when you're still feeling pleased to have been published, regardless of the quality of the other

poems in the book, you get another order form. Your work has been specially selected to be read on a tape by a professional actor. Only the best material from the anthology has been selected for this treatment. If you want to order a copy of the tape, it will only cost you ...

8. Further suggestions arrive at regular intervals. You could have a copy of your poem presented in a beautiful wooden frame. You could even have a certificate acknowledging its quality, with a copy of the poem attached to it. You could have the poem displayed on the Internet for the world to read ...

Seen enough? You will have realised by now why we said that poetry is preferred for this type of anthology comp because of its brevity. The fact that six poems can be printed on an A4 page means that there are six chances of poets willing to buy all the merchandising from which the organisers profit. It's not surprising they can afford to attract you with offers of free entry into the competition.

One thing we must stress is that this type of anthology comp is legal. You may not feel that it is particularly ethical, but there is nothing to prevent the organisers from running competitions in this way every month of the year ... and they might well do that if people enter in sufficient numbers and buy all the products as suggested. And, of course, there is nothing to stop other businessmen from jumping on the bandwagon and adapting the anthology comp practices to suit their own purposes.

Sheep and goat division

It is extremely difficult to know how satisfactory any comp is unless you've had first hand experience of it. Even then, you may not be sure about areas of its organisation. Here are a few tips that might help.

1. Suspect anything that's free, unless you are familiar with its name and reputation. For example, plenty of first rate

179

women's magazines run short story competitions as an outlet for their readers. The comp brings the magazine good publicity, awards prizes and associated kudos to the winners, and can even supplement its own stable of regular writers by "talent spotting" and approaching the writers of the best stories to commission work from them. There is seldom an entry fee, although you might have to buy the magazine to obtain an entry coupon. The familiar names and reputations of these publications will assure you that they're above reproach.

If, however, the organiser is somebody you've never heard of at an address you don't know, and is offering huge prizes and free entry, you are right to be suspicious. Why not get in touch and find out a little more? You could ask if it's the first comp the organiser has run. If not, ask for details of winners from previous occasions. Ask whether previous anthologies are available for inspection. Check with writer friends or, if you don't know any, ask the reference library if they can put you in touch with any local writers. You may find that you are dealing with a perfectly legitimate organisation, but if things do not turn out so well, you could be very glad that you checked up.

2. Find out how many winning and/or shortlisted pieces are going to appear in the anthology. If it's more than a dozen or so stories (or a few more if they're very short) or over sixty poems, be very wary.

3. Check that writers whose work features in the anthology will be given courtesy copies. (Don't expect a handful of them – few competitions arrange for those with work in the anthology to receive more than one free copy.)

4. Check that writers in the anthology retain all further copyright on their material.

At the end of the day, you can't be certain of everything and you have to trust someone. Our advice is to have a go – and if you find yourself at the mercy of a business anthologist determined to rip you off, refuse to be ripped. Don't waste your precious time and creative energy agonising over what you should have done. You don't have to patronise that particular comp again. Simply go on to the next competition, where you're likely to encounter fair treatment.

As in all walks of life, the goodies outweigh the baddies. Most competitions are genuine, fun, mutually beneficial affairs. And the anthologies of winning entries are a pleasing outlet for your successful writing. The problem is that the baddies get more publicity. But the world of writing competitions is just too big, exciting and exhilarating for you to risk sacrificing the joy of entering simply because you're afraid of the minority who may not treat you well.

Closing thought

As football commentators might well tell you: *writing is a funny old game.* Every writer's career goes through highs and lows. And it's possible to lose confidence, especially if you are finding it difficult to dream up fresh ideas, the words won't flow and the postie has just brought you another clutch of rejected manuscripts. (Yours – not his!)

Sometimes you can doubt you ever had any talent. Could you ever write? Or did you just imagine it?

That's when having a pile of anthologies is a life saver. Being able to have a look through your old winners will quickly raise your spirits. It helps get the bad patch into perspective. You realise that it's just an arid phase. It'll pass. The magic is still there, waiting to be unleashed.

Even if you are doing well, it's entertaining to dig out old anthologies a few years on and reread your work. You will probably wince at what you entered back then. It's nothing compared to the jewels you produce now. You'll be able to see how much more polished and sophisticated your technique, style, command of language and imagery have become.

So enjoy your anthology. It's great to cuddle up to on a long winter's night. It'll still keep you warm long after the winning cheque – and the memory of it – have faded away!

12

THE MAGIC TOUCH

Right – by this point in the book we wouldn't blame you if you thought the time for talking was over. We've hit you with every hint, tip, piece of advice and warning we can think of. And we've offered a host of different techniques for turning out a winning entry.

You've had all the theory – what catches a judge's eye, what makes him groan in disgust and what special elements blend together to create a truly memorable entry.

It's all good stuff and useful too – but we suspect you're yearning for us to shut up and show you the real thing, the genuine article (and short story and poem)! You're hissing: *enough of concepts, ideas and techniques – show us some winners. Let's actually read some prize-grabbing entries.*

Okay, who are we to deny you? Here is a selection of pieces which have won prizes in major competitions. They're all very different in style, tempo and approach, but they share one common thread – the writers who submitted them all had the magic touch.

Read each twice – once just for enjoyment then a second time to analyse what makes the piece work, what makes it special, what singled it out from the mass. See what techniques the authors have used to cast a seductive spell. Experience them for yourself.

You may not like them all. That's okay. Remember, writing is a subjective business – and even judges can't always agree on what is good – but each item has a little something that makes it worth your attention. See if you can spot that special ingredient too. If you can, then we suggest you're well on your way to creating your own stunning work.

After each piece we'll give a few paragraphs of comment explaining what made the work appeal to us. See if you agree with our opinions. We'll start with short stories, then poems and articles. All set? Right, here we go – have fun.

SECTION ONE: SHORT STORIES

The Case of the Doctor's Dilemma
by Steve Teasdale

"Tell me what you see, my dear friend." Holmes' voice held the note of triumph which Doctor Watson recognised from many previous cases. He peered through the microscope lens and gave a small shrug of annoyance.

"Powder?" he ventured.

"No, no old chap. The trained mind must deal in specifics," Holmes lectured. "Be precise!"

"Grey powder?" Watson guessed.

"Ash!" the great detective pronounced with a well-cultivated air of smugness. "Sample 'A' is cigarette ash. A fine Turkish blend, hand rolled by Hedges and Company at their excellent emporium in Knightsbridge. The very brand smoked by the late Sir Willoughby Fanshawe-Brunt, no less."

"That's all very well, Holmes," Watson retorted, "but the man died from a dagger in the back – not nicotine poisoning!"

"Just so," Holmes agreed. "A dagger wielded by a left handed man of below average height. The butler is only five feet tall, left handed and, more to the point, smokes cheap Dutch Cigars. A more discerning eye than yours would have noticed that the sample of ash labelled 'B' is of Dutch East Indian origin and was found by the body!"

"Balderdash," said Watson. "It could just as easily have been the French maid. She's a slip of a thing ... and hated poor old Sir Willoughby to boot!"

"Your logic is flawed, dear fellow," Sherlock Holmes said, as if instructing a child. "Name me one woman who smokes shilling cigars."

"Mrs Hudson." The good doctor was pleased to see he'd rattled his room mate and tapped the side of his nose knowingly. "I'm always finding half smoked butts in the strangest places. Why bless my soul if she isn't becoming a regular nicotine fiend in her old age."

Holmes reached for his trusty violin, but stayed his hand at the look of pained dismay that flitted across his tone deaf companion's face. Instead, he settled into his favourite armchair and proceeded to deflate the doctor's supposition.

"A reasonable assumption, Watson," he said, "but an erroneous one for all that. A man of much sharper intellect – a man such as I – would observe several facts. Firstly, Mrs Hudson's teeth. The woman has a disconcerting habit of leaving her dentures in the bathroom, and they are gleaming white – not yellowed by smoke. Then there is the matter of just where the cigar butts appear. Several I have observed about the back door, and one or two upon the third floor landing outside Mrs Hudson's own room. These points, coupled with the fact that our food bills have recently diminished led me to the real solution. Dear old Mrs Hudson is having it away with Mr Monke the butcher!"

Watson gasped at his friend's brilliant grasp of the facts and flopped into his own chair. "I say, but that's a rum do, Holmes. I always thought the old gel fancied Inspector Lestrade!"

"Who can account for human nature, old friend," Holmes said, lighting his pipe. "Why, take you for example, Watson. We've been close companions for twelve years and you still think you can hide things from me."

Watson made a fuff-fuffing noise peculiar to retired Indian Army officers and tugged at his mutton chop whiskers. "Damned if I know what you mean, old fella!" he blustered.

Holmes smiled tolerantly at his rotund friend's obvious discomfort. "Come, come, my good doctor. Let us look at this morning's peculiar chain of events. You arose at six o'clock precisely and spent several minutes pruning your whiskers."

"Pure conjecture," Watson said, falling into the expected pattern which allowed Holmes to develop his ideas.

"Not so," the great detective replied. "After serving as chief medical officer to the Bengal Rifle Brigade for fifteen years you are conditioned to waking at six – with or without a bugle call. And as for the other matter, I could not help but notice small curls of male hair around the wash basin."

"What of it?" Watson demanded. "Can't a fella take pride in his appearance without a chap studying his chin stubble?"

"Such vanity," Holmes said with a mocking smile. "And I suggest that it was this self same vanity which led you to conceal the following events from me!"

"Don't know what'cha mean, I'm sure," Watson bristled.

"Then you deny that a messenger boy called on you at exactly eleven minutes past nine?" Holmes was gratified to see the look of admiration flit across Watson's face. "I heard his tread upon the stair at precisely that time and, judging from the noise his trousers failed to make, deduced he was a messenger."

"Nonsense," Watson said. "What possible significance can *quiet* trousers have?"

"The current fashion is for wide bottomed apparel, which flap noisily when walking. Your visitor made no such noise, which means he was either trouserless – an unlikely notion at best – or else he was wearing bicycle clips. Who but a mounted messenger from that most esteemed periodical *The Strand Magazine* would be so equipped?"

Watson's jaw dropped in amazement. "By the Lord Harry, Holmes, you are spot on! But how could you tell *where* the chap was from?"

"Elementary, my dear Watson," Holmes explained. You left the empty envelope at the breakfast table. It is of a particular buff manila with a watermark peculiar to the stationers in High Holborn frequented by the admirable editor of the *Strand*. Furthermore, your name was on the front, written in a style of copperplate taught at better public schools. Is not the editor a former pupil of Winchester? Expelled in 1879 for plagiarism – if memory serves me well."

"Good Lord!" Watson shook his head in disbelief. "Next thing, you'll be telling me what was in the damned thing."

"Ah, now *that* is easy," Holmes replied. "Though I am at a loss as to why your latest story has been rejected."

"Now you're guessing," Watson said.

"Deducing – not guessing," Holmes demurred. "The envelope is too large for the usual five guinea cheque you receive for each well penned story. As I proof read all your tales of my cases the thing has not been returned for correction. So I conclude that you have been rejected, my poor fellow – a serious blow to your vanity!"

"Bravo!" Watson clapped in open hero worship. "As usual, you have solved the puzzle."

"But for one point," said Holmes. "Why the rejection?"

"A trifling matter, old boy," Watson assured the world's greatest detective investigator. "The editor believes that I have drawn your character too sympathetically. He claims that for a chap to be so absolutely spot on at detective work is simply not realistic."

"Not realistic?" Holmes sucked at his pipe furiously.

"He wants me to make you more believable," Watson explained. "You know – a bit of love interest, or have you make a mistake."

Holmes leapt to his feet and jammed his deerstalker onto his head. "Sherlock Holmes is never wrong!" he cried. "Give me that damnable story – I'll return it in person and have a word with this ... this ... upstart!"

Watson stared open mouthed as the cleverest known human in the British Empire – perhaps in the whole civilised world – stormed off on his mission of retribution.

Mrs Hudson came bustling up the stairs, a look of servile working class concern on her face. "Why, bless me soul, Doctor Watson! I ain't never seen Mister 'Olmes in such a to-do and never you mind. He fair put me on my back, and no mistake!"

"It's that damned editor of mine," Watson explained. "The idiot actually suggested poor Holmes might one day make a mistake!"

"Calm yourself," Mrs Hudson fussed, reaching into the pocket of her pinafore. "Have a cigar. A good smoke always unwinds me!"

This hilarious yarn is a wickedly perceptive pastiche. It succeeded in the double whammy of not only making the judge laugh out loud, but cleverly sending up the many absurdities of Sherlock Holmes stories.

Conan Doyle's hero may be the most famous detective in fiction but he's also an unbelievably irritating know-it-all. This fondly mocking parody shows up Holmes for the insufferably smug, pompous bore that he unquestionably is.

There's sheer delight for the reader in seeing him being tripped up by his own arrogance. It's a comeuppance that's long overdue!

Steve Teasdale's story has great wit and comic timing, but it also has an air of authenticity. The conversation between

Holmes and Watson could have come straight from Conan Doyle's pen and has a wonderfully Victorian period feel. A clever satire, well executed.

The Moon's Finger
by Vivien Wright

I buried my nose in the thick coarse wool of my father's jumper. I loved its comforting familiar smell of fish, tar and a grown man's sweat.

"You cold, child?"

I nodded. He put his arm round me and lifted me on to his lap, pulling his heavy cloth coat so that it enveloped us both. I snuggled up, desperately loving him.

We were sitting in the shelter of the dunes, watching, waiting. There was no moon, hidden as it was behind the lowering bank of cloud. The sea was inky black, with a white fringe just visible at the edge of the water. The only sound was the soft sucking of the waves as they ebbed and flowed up on to the thin band of shingle.

I felt sick with excitement. At last, at long last, I was to be the one on the dune. How clearly I remembered my eighth birthday when I had pleaded with both Pa and Ma to let me be the one but they had looked at each other in that certain way and said I was much too young and irresponsible. For the whole of the next year I had tried so hard, striving to remember to do everything I had been told, just as well as I could. Pa knew I was desperate to please him, to let him see he could rely on me. On my ninth birthday he had sat in his usual chair by the fire and called me to him. His eyes had smiled at me from under his bushy eyebrows as I stood in front of him. He had cupped my small hands in his huge rope-roughened fingers.

"You're a good girl, Josie. You're growing up into a fine lass and I'm proud of you. Just a little more mindfulness now and you'll soon be there."

I had struggled to hold back my tears. I knew he had not forgotten when my dreaming had nearly lost us our cow in the dyke.

And now I was ten. Just three hours ago we had been sitting together in the lee of Pa's boat, letting the dry sand sift through our fingers and enjoying the last gleams of the evening sun. I had snuggled against him as I always did, loving him, warm in his protection. I had always treasured those quiet moments with my father, just him and me and the sea. His voice had broken the comfortable silence, unfamiliar, tight with tension.

"Josie, it's tonight."

The hairs on the back of my neck crawled.

"Tonight you are to stand on the dune. You'll be holding the lives of our men in your hands. Don't let them down."

The dry sand had stopped flowing, the sharp grains cutting into my skin as my nails dug into my palms. I could only whisper, "I won't, Pa, I won't let you down."

In the long silent wait in the dunes with Pa, my excitement began to ebb. The darkness was thick, the only light a luminescence from the edge of the water. I struggled to keep my eyes open but his warmth and the hypnotic rhythm of the sea lulled me to sleep.

"Josie! It's time."

He was whispering, shaking me.

"Look at the flares, over there."

In the darkness towards Southwold was a tiny flicker of light. Then another, nearer, brighter. As each one flared and died, so the next leapt into life. I knew all the secret places where the men were hidden, they, like us, waiting in the tense silence. The torches carried the message quickly down the coast, Southwold, Walberswick, Dunwich. It was now. They'd gone, the Excise men were gone!

"Run, Josie. It's time."

Although it was the blackest of nights, the path to the cottage was as familiar to me as the lines on my own hand. Gasping with fear and excitement I pushed through the still marram grass, soundlessly slid down the dry dunes and ran to the muddy creek.

"It's time, Ma. The flares a' been."

She quickly lit the candle and I followed Ma up the stairs to the wide attic room. In the corner hugging the chimney breast, a tiny triangular window had been set into the roof. It was the smallest window I had ever seen, made of thick glass that bulged like that in my father's telescope. It had always puzzled me, that little hidden window. I had walked round and round the cottage staring up at the roof but could never find it. It was only when I went to the sea that I could see it, winking at me as the sun caught its pane. Ma's hand trembled as she put the candle on the shelf in front of the window.

"Now off you go, Josie and don't you take your eyes off this candle for even a minute. There's a lot of folks depends on you tonight."

I could hear the soft clink of tack and the whispered shouts even before I got to the beach. It was alive with men and horses, struggling and slipping in the soft sand. Lanterns were held aloft and from the darkness of the sea came a muffled sound of oars. They were coming!

I stood where Pa had told me to stand, on top of the dunes so I could see back across the marshes to the cottage and down towards The Gap. I could see Ma's candle in the window, its light hugely magnified by the thick glass. I watched the light as long as I could but the excitement on the beach was tempting. Many hands were helping to pull the boat into the shallow water. The packets and barrels were quickly lifted out and passed along the human chain stretching up the beach to the restless packhorses.

The eerie silence was broken only by the soft whinnying of a waiting animal. I could see Pa up to his knees in the water, lifting great bundles above his head and passing them to the next man. How proud I was of him.

I remembered Ma and the candle. Turning, I looked into the darkness.

Darkness! Where was the candle? How long had it been out? A horse whinnied. Not from the beach but from the rough track leading to our cottage. Panic-stricken I rushed down the sand and into the water pulling at Pa's coat.

"The candle, Pa. It's gone out."

A rough hand clamped my mouth shut.

"Stop your yelling, girl, get back in the dunes and lie quiet."

With one word from Pa, packets were tossed back into the boat and the muffled oars began their silent work, melting the small boat into the blackness. Now I could hear the jingling of horses, the hard sound of their hooves changing to a soft regular thud as they left the stony track and turned on to the marshy path beside our cottage. Oh, hurry hurry, they'll be here. Why hadn't I watched for the light as I had been told?

Quickly the laden horses were led in all directions, some, I knew, to become part of the shadows in the pines along the edge of the marshes, others to slip along the maze of hidden paths beneath the levees of the dykes. In moments Pa was standing there, motionless, alone, on the beach.

Two horses, their riders tall and upright, were silhouetted against the clouds as they reached the break in the dunes. They were so near to me that I could smell the rancid sweat of the horses and the leather of their saddles. I heard one of the riders gasp as he saw Pa. There was a sharp exchange of words then shouting as the big horses circled roughly around him. I lay still as death then saw in horror a long finger of moonlight edging along the beach. The tide was turning and taking with it the dark clouds.

As the pale light reached Pa all the work of the night could be seen, the hoof marks, the footprints, the scuffs in the sand where the barrels had been dragged, a package dropped in the hurry to flee. With a triumphant laugh the Excise man lifted his crop and caught Pa across the face, ripping open his cheek. As he fell to the ground I screamed and ran down the beach. Terrified by my sudden noise, the horse reared up, high above me. Then his hooves crashed straight down on to Pa's head, crushing him awkwardly into the sand. He lay quite still, dark blood beginning to ooze from the curved imprint on the side of his head.

"Pa!" I shrieked. "Wake up."

I touched his face but he didn't move. I shook him but his head rolled over so that the hard grains of sand poured into his open eyes. Frantically, I tried to turn his head, brushing the sand away from his dear face, my salty tears falling in his rough hair. I kissed him, calling "Pa, Pa," over and over again. But he didn't stir.

Shaking with fear, I put my cheek close to his mouth as he had showed me to do with the new born calf. I expected to feel his breath, warm and regular, just like the calf. But no breath came from him and I knew that my beloved Pa was dead.

And I knew that I had held his life in my hands and had killed him by my unmindfulness.

The Excise man looked down at me but I could not move, frozen by the horror of seeing my beloved Pa lying there.

"That's a quicker way than hanging," was all he said.

This is storytelling at its most powerful. The plot of The Moon's Finger is simple and fairly straightforward and in lesser hands would have been unremarkable, but Vivien Wright's stunning descriptions lift this historical tale to another level. She creates a magical sense of setting and era.

The reader is whisked straight back in time to a century of smugglers and Excise Men, a time of lawlessness and adventure where quick and violent death lurks around every corner.

Her descriptions not only recreate this dangerous world in minute detail but help build a feeling of mood and menace. The atmosphere is dark and brooding. The story ripples with tension.

What especially marks this story as a winner is the ending. It is downbeat, quiet, restrained – almost throwaway – but somehow that makes it all the more shocking. Death is shown as being commonplace – a casual but brutal event. The cruel humour of the Excise man can't fail to stun and repel the reader.

Space Cadet
by Kerry Hood-Edwards

The gate fell off. He was for it, even though it wasn't his fault. The gate had simply swooned like a creaky-booted guardsman overheating on parade.

With eyes narrowed, tongue stabbing the corner of his mouth and rough fingers tracing newish hinges, he could only crouch over the unconscious soldier. Picking at the splintered gloss paint like an elbow scab, he poured himself a picture of Natalie Tickle's red nails. (His 'below average' end-of-term assessment had cited Allows Mind To Wander.)

Natalie Tickle's red nails were worth wandering over, despite their splintered gloss paint. He had loved her from their first fateful placing in the Infants – just out of pudding spoon reach – until she had become a mere mortal and moved in next door.

Even now, there were moments: Natalie Tickle in a bikini; lisping to Westlife; stroking her spastic rabbit, red nails splattered across its twitchy fur like multiple gunshots. Those moments warp-nined her from the Nearly Lumpy Vest Years to the blonde one out of All Saints. Natalie Tickle was ten.

He'd drunk enough of her and burped. Time to sort out the gate, to use the elimination method his father, an AA man, had started to teach him. "Gatepost: check."

"Check."

"Hasp. Hinges. Horizontal hold. Hula Hoops."

"Dad!"

"Check?"

"Check."

The gate had fallen off and it wasn't his fault. Even so, he was for it.

"Chicken nuggets. Fish fingers." The question disguised as a statement came from his mother; she hadn't turned when he entered the kitchen, but froze, hip pushed out and arms wide like a crucified grocer, weighing grey minced bird against grey minced fish.

"Chicken ... finger-nuggets," he said and bit his lip, waiting. But she only sighed, a three-part in ... and out; bra top rising ... and blotting sweat from her shoulder blades. True, he wasn't funny, but his friends would have laughed and called him Tosser and done that thing with the right hand that he sort of understood.

But here was a silence louder than waiting for the head to walk into assembly, so he looked for a diversion among the stack of cardboard boxes. They were moving out, probably. He still didn't know.

They'd only moved in three years before, on his seventh birthday. He remembered unwrapping newspapered things and pretending they were presents; then he broke a mirror and his mother screamed, which made him run down the garden and hide under the bush that had bunches of petals like cauliflowers. (His mother: following with plasters, just in case; pulling him out of the petals, kissing his wet face. His father: chasing him with inky hands around the spinning washing-line; making roary noises; making him laugh until he got the hiccups.)

Now they were moving out again, probably. He counted the boxes. They had lies written all over them and only he could memorise this information onto his Sub-Cranial Scanner and Mind-Meld it to his team of Extra-Terrestrial Code-Breakers.

Wagon Wheels, Twelve Packets: check. Chirpy Cheap Shop Panty Pads (With Wings), Thirty: check. Time to tell her about the gate.

"Can I empty the bin?" he asked. He wondered if all summer holidays would smell like that now, not of boat oil or cherryade or wet barbecues, but of old spring onions poking through a bin liner.

"Can I empty ..."

"Leave it." The back of her head moved; he scanned the black hair for the silver one. It had moved house, probably.

Unless she was a Replicant. It did happen, and his mother was thirty-five – old for a Humanoid – although her face wasn't due to fall off until she was forty or forty-one, like Natalie Tickle's mother, who'd been around a lot lately. He didn't want his mind wandering over Natalie Tickle's mother because her eyes bulged and she had the sort of nose that got stuck in wine glasses. Worse, she enjoyed telling him he had to be Grown-Up, peppering his hair with glossy red gunshots and calling him a Regular Shirley Temple, as if he came with Regular Fries.

Then the Ancient Humanoids would send him into the garden while they spoke the language of their mother-ship: tutting like kangaroos; moving their mouths with no sound coming out. (Which he'd seen done better in pantomime.)

Still, better in the garden than inside with the Mothers speaking without tongues; waiting for him to leave. Just because his father had *Left.*

The fridge clinked; dry ice tiptoed from the low freezer around his mother's legs, making him remember Ch'ado Gori, Intergalactic Space Cadet, Actual Size Twenty-Eight Point Five Centimetres. Ch'ado Gori had beetle-like armour, silver cape, yellow rubber hair and a purple button between his legs. When you pressed it, the rubber hair flipped back and sprayed Futuro-Fantastic Force Fog, fatal to Pimp, Black-Haired Intergalactic Space Cadet.

It worked too; he borrowed Martin Potter's and vaporised Natalie Tickle's Barbie, then blasted her gerbil off its wheel towards impalement on the water bottle.

Ch'ado Gori had been advertised in a Sunday supplement, the price in dollars, his mother in 'you can't have everything' mode and the magazine going to line her half-empty chest of drawers. He didn't want everything, because that would have to include tomatoes and waistcoats. His father only had a sports bag when he *Left*.

Which wasn't much, he thought, not when you see all the boxes that didn't have Wagon Wheels or Panty Pads in them, but were full of his father's things. Of his father.

His mother hadn't turned around. Any second now, the frozen hand of Pimp, Black-Haired Intergalactic Space Cadet, was going to grab her pimply arm and drag her into the mixed veg.

There was hair under her arms and, for the first time, he was embarrassed, wished he could look away. But it was a different sort of curiosity to when he'd caught his parents in the shower. Then, he'd only had to work out why Privates had Public Hair. Which he put to his father, who told him about sex and said that with so many questions he was going to be a Right Philosopher (he still might be if he learned to spell it, and if it meant you always got a straight answer like that).

In his room, he had his own T.V. and Video. He wouldn't have minded sometimes watching with his mother downstairs, even *Wimbledon* or *Gardening Things*. They could sit on the sofa.

But he always felt in the way downstairs, so he watched *Carry On* films on satellite. It sounds louder, he thought, when you laugh on your own, but quieter after horror videos, when you daren't go across the landing to the toilet and have to hold it in all night.

She had warned him about Aids and someone called Perverts or Evil People – "Go and wash your hands," she was saying now into the freezer – but he already knew about Aids from the Internet. And there was no way someone called Evil People was going to get him. He turned the tap on and off and sat at the table. No way. And if this Perverts mush tried marching him down a tunnel to torture him on a dirty zed-bed, he'd kick him in the purple button, flip his head back, stun him with Supra-Calibre-Frag-Elastic Futuro-Fantastic Force Fog and blow his goolies away.

"Properly," his mother said into the egg shelf, so he went back to the sink and brushed the towel across his hands, trying to work it out; how he had to be Grown-Up, yet felt twenty-eight point five centimetres high, with body parts inspected and controlled by a bigger cadet with all-seeing, invisible eyes; how his mother warned him about Aids and Perverts and Evil People, but couldn't tell him his father was dead.

There was a new boy at school called Amjei, whose parents got him from Sainsbury's. It was true: Amjei had shown him the receipt. On the back it said: 'Phone This Number to Foster or Adopt: Kent Social Services'. He'd better be good or they might exchange him for baby carrots.

If you could get a replacement parent from Sainsbury's, he thought, holding the ketchup upside down, dad would be with the peas. "Two peas in a pod," the man at the yard had said when they bought wood for the tree-house. The tree-house was never finished. Sometimes, he sat under the big petals, waiting to be pulled out.

He wasn't stupid; his father wasn't in Sainsbury's; he knew exactly where he was. "Your father," was all his mother had said, "has *Left*".

Yet, he was taken to the cemetery; if his father had *Left*, what was he doing down there and what did playing squash have to do with it?

Later, The Awful Truth Dawned. (He'd got that from a CD-ROM book and resented all the energy he'd put into not telling lies, when the truth was going to be awful anyway.) And it hadn't come at dawn, but at night, after *Zombie Grave Robbers*.

The ketchup had plopped into its lid, but his tea wasn't ready, so he looked under the table and smiled at Ch'ado Gori, on long-term loan from Martin Potter and now saluting the chair-legs. Suddenly, his mother turned, slid a plate across the table and slumped opposite.

"Your eyes are red," he said, adding bravely, "and you've got your elbows on the table."

She started laughing and crying and gasping as loud as he had when a jellyfish from hell got his big toe. He stared, then went over but she shoved him away into the box marked Panty Pads (With Wings), Thirty. Snot was running into her mouth. She looked twenty-eight point five centimetres high and all he could do was run in circles, flapping his fingers and wanting the toilet.

"What do I do, what do I do?" he dribbled. They were both screaming. He didn't know any phone numbers, except for Kent Social Services and Sainsbury's.

She must have found out about the gate. He was saying sorry but his throat had stalled. Reaching under the table, he offered

Ch'ado Gori, Intergalactic Space Cadet, due to earn his first stripe. His mother shook her head; he insisted, but she snatched it from him, shouting "I don't want it. I don't want your stupid toy. Why can't you leave me alone?"

She was heaving, wheezing and coughing. Water, he thought. He'd seen an old war film where some American was dying all moody in a lifeboat, then drank a flask of water and the next thing, he was in bed with clean pyjamas, smoking cigars.

She was still mumbling about his stupid toys, his stupid everythings. He poured some water. Suddenly, Ch'ado Gori, Intergalactic Space Cadet, flew across the room, knocking the mug from his fat rough fingers.

The kitchen started to glow. He was sweating and felt sick trying to vacuum air up his nose while blowing Force Fog out of it. Now his head stung. Intergalactic Space Cadets were fearless, cool and tanned. He would make his father proud.

All the same, a rumble travelled from his sandals to his knees, over his groin, past his belly button and along his ribs, pulsing his throat until it burst through his teeth with a Juvenile Humanoid:

"Mm..uu...mm!"

He was on his back on the floor, clutching Ch'ado Gori, Intergalactic Space Cadet. His mother was leaning over him. She was still crying, but in a way he recognised, saying his name and looking at him, her tears trailing his face; whispering Anger Is Only Natural When Someone Dies; promising Everything Is Going To Be Alright. She must have seen his CD-ROM, although he was more inclined to believe her version. She couldn't Make It All Better. His father was dead and not even Ch'ado Gori was going to get him out of that one.

Even so, he and his mother had been acting out *Night of the Living Dead* when all the time she had the power to cure them both. Whatever medicine she'd just rubbed into her hands, it was working. He had to tell her about the gate.

"It fell off," he said, still lying flat. "The gate just fell off," and they both knew he'd kicked it in.

This is a challenging – some might even say difficult – story and its selection as a prize-winner did provoke a certain amount of controversy. *But although Space Cadet is a yarn which requires a little extra effort, concentration and interpretation by the reader, its unconventional style is exciting and dynamic.*

Kerry Hood-Edwards is clearly trying to strike out in new directions and produces a highly skilful and moving piece of storytelling in the process. It is harsh, but poignant; painful but upbeat.

Judged by any standards this is a clever, emotionally-gripping, bitter-sweet short story. But the two aspects of the tale that particularly impress are the chillingly accurate portrayal of the grief-stricken adults wandering around in a daze, whispering to each other, unsure what to do or what to tell the day-dreaming ten-year old boy who has just lost his father; and the touching description of the mother's numbness and short temper.

You can sense the tension twisting within her, building to boiling point as she goes about everyday tasks in an anger-filled trance, her life now robbed of all meaning.

What made this story stand out is the unorthodox and thought-provoking use of imagery. The writer makes us see normally mundane background details in a whole new light.

Happy Hills
by Adam Brown

Since taking the unselfish decision to vacate our small house, and avail himself of the 'superb care and facilities' of the 'exquisitely located Happy Hills Rest Home' (I have the brochure before me) – my disgraced father has become something of a golf fanatic. My father! Golf! Just imagining the old dog padding around on the greens plays havoc with my circulation.

Quite simply, the thought offends me. Nothing previously in his life had suggested the late flowering of such a gentlemanly pursuit. It appears, though, that his autumnal years have finally brought some of the social ambition so lacking in his prime. (As for etiquette, I doubt he ever knew the meaning of the word, decorum never having been his strong suit.) My father! Golf! I *cannot* swallow it. It cannot be true. But true it is. As Trudi says, "Why did he wait so long?"

I still blush furiously at my lapse in self control the day I found out. In a clumsy display of paternal empathy he'd sent a letter directly to my own club. I was in the Members' Lounge, sharing a quiet, post-Medal Ruddles with Colin Holmes, the club secretary, when I opened it.

"Letters to the club, eh? Not your bit on the side I trust?" Colin chuckled into his beer.

"No ... it's er ... nothing," I mumbled, recognising the scrawl immediately.

"Ah ... righto ..."

Colin must have sensed my embarrassment, because he turned to another table, leaving me to my reading. Bemused, I glanced over the shakily written contents of his missive. My eye was caught by the following:

"I would of told you before, but wasn't sure how you'd react. What a game Davey! I can see why you spend so much time at it. Maybe we could play together some time? I could come down to you for a weekend praps."

What, and wipe out the sins of a lifetime in one fell swoop? Praps not.

I can't remember precisely at which point I knocked my pint of Ruddles into Colin's lap, though I recall vividly the distasteful look on his face as he asked Cindy for a cloth. My apologies were as sincere as they were profuse, and Colin, after cleaning himself up, smiled and asked me what on earth was 'up'. Clearly a credible explanation was called for, and fortunately, my powers of improvisation obliged. I've no idea where the idea came from. It just flashed into my mind. I told him that there'd been a death in the family. It was a half truth, I suppose. Now it was Colin's turn to be embarrassed.

"Oh I say ... I'm ... I am sorry Dave ... Really ... One never knows what to ... "

"Don't worry. Just an old uncle. I hardly knew him."

The matter finished there. I was sure, however, that my chances of the up-coming vice-captaincy, hitherto almost a certainty, were blown to the wind, and I resolved to avoid any further contact with the lifelong cause of my shame. Besides, the idea of him visiting my club, in whatever state of reformation, made me shudder.

Colin left me to my thoughts: "Better get these off – don't want the old fella catching a chill!" And the nightmare of father's last visit flooded back. The kids crying. Trudi running into my study, muttering about a dirty tramp on the doorstep, and could I deal with it. Inebriated, homeless, and scarcely able to walk, he'd stood pitifully before me.

"Take me in Davey. Please, I've nothing."

What could I do? What *can* one do? And we did have a spare room.

"A day or two," I said grudgingly, "till you get yourself sorted out." After a week Trudi stopped speaking to me. I decided he had to go, and went up to his room to break the news. Despite my anger, I didn't relish the moment. He snivelled like a baby for a while, and a surge of pity welled up in me. Then he had the nerve to call me a snob.

*   *   *

There are times when one's conscience takes on battles it is simply not up to; and this, I'm afraid, was one of those times. The word 'father' had all but lost its meaning for me, and yet ... and yet ... the bond of blood is hard to sunder. No matter how much it has already been weakened by unhappy circumstance.

I have never examined, too closely, my feelings on the subject – a mix of shame, resentment and good, old-fashioned self-preservation would probably come close. And I've done well. I'm doing all right, no thanks to *father*.

When he turned up on my doorstep, I hadn't seen him for a dozen or so years. All I'd heard were one or two alarming reports from an ancient aunt, and these hadn't exactly fanned the flames of filial love. Who wants to know that one's father has gone to the dogs, after all? Not a happily married management consultant; snob or no snob.

We honestly couldn't have kept him. His uncouthness would have tried a saint. And I'm no saint. Besides he was, at this stage, more or less completely bed-ridden – some arterial thing – and I felt that professional help might be more appropriate. Trudi took the children away. On her mother's advice I made a few phone calls, to see if anyone could take him.

We were fortunate. Happy Hills had space. Plus, they didn't charge an arm and a leg. I took him up there the next day. Gave him some cash to keep him happy. He'd been with us a fortnight, which felt like a decade. The house smelt of rotting flesh.

*   *   *

Three weeks after the Ruddles incident, to my surprise and delight, I got voted in as VC after all, and, taking time-out from a bubbly celebration at home, found myself drunkenly rereading father's letter. I realised I hadn't even finished it the first time, and a wave of guilt swept over me. His enthusiasm for the glorious game was really quite touching. It even provided him with a social life, something altogether absent during his wilderness years. I was mildly puzzled as to how he'd suddenly found the stamina to complete a full round of golf. The answer came in the final paragraph:

"It's a beautiful little course, just the right length for an old fellow like me. I've only made it as far as 12 so far, 13's a killer! Bob hasn't hit the green in years of trying. Only a par 3 mind, a little island in a lake. When the wind's up, you can't even get close. I reckon you could manage it Davey."

So he gave up after twelve. Hardly a round of golf. Still, not bad for someone in his condition. In fact, he must have made a miraculous recovery since his short stay with us. The last time I'd seen his legs, they were a foul greyish colour.

Reading on, in the diminished light of the study, I found my eyes slowly moistening. I realised I'd really been something of a cad, whisking him off as I had. And I'd not been up once to visit. The old man was plainly making a last ditch attempt to enter the long neglected corridors of respectability. He described his difficulties in mastering the fast greens – *"I blame the putter Davey"* – and even spoke of trying to acquire a handicap, the irony of which mortified me.

After a lifetime of mindless afternoons, misspent in betting shops and pubs; nights trawling the streets; mornings waking up God only knew where, he was finally coming good. And how had I responded? His last remaining kin, the person he'd most wanted to impress with his reformed twilight existence. I might as well have said, I don't care if you live or die.

*   *   *

Fetching my treasured antique putter from the garage, I climb into the car. Colin's silhouette twirls with Trudi's in the lounge window. Soon they will all want to toast my success – the youngest VC since the War. They will call for me to speak. They will look everywhere. They will not find me. The Surrey landscape races by. When I made the journey with father eighteen months ago it took an eternity.

"I know I've not been a good father to you Davey. Now we've something to share in my final years."

Standing humbly outside the drab Victorian rest home, clutching the damp remnants of his letter, I ask myself what kind of a son I've been?

When I explain who I am, the night nurse is surprised, not to say a little hostile.

"Rather a strange time to make your first visit," she mutters sarcastically.

"Yes I know, I ... It is a little ... I ... er ... hadn't expected ..."

"You didn't even call to see how the operation went," she adds dismissively. "The poor man nearly died."

My mind flounders in the disinfected silence (operation, what operation?) and I struggle to maintain a semblance of propriety.

"I ... couldn't get here any sooner. Things have ... How is he now?"

"Better than he was. He was in intensive for six weeks."

"Exactly how long ago was the er ... operation?"

"About four months." Four months. From her accusing eyes shines the judgement of the world.

"I know it's late ... I have something for him."

She casts a skeptical eye at my unwrapped gift. The old and trustworthy blade, with which I am about to part.

"You'd better come with me."

I know something isn't right as soon as I enter the room. The bed maybe, where he lies motionless. I switch on the lamp.

"Father," I whisper. He stirs. He looks older than I've ever seen him. Smaller too. Slowly his eyelids part.

"Davey, my boy! Sit down! I thought you'd never ..." There's no chair. I place myself awkwardly on the edge of the bed.

"The nurse says you've had an operation." He looks away sheepishly.

"Ah that was months ago. I'm all right now, son."

"Was it serious?"

"No no, not too bad. The old artery thing. Right as rain now."

"I mean er ... do you ... can you still play? I've ... brought this for you." The sight of the ancient putter brings a smile to his face, which rapidly turns into a grin. He reaches down beside him and picks up a slim grey plastic case, which he places on the bed before him. Mechanically he opens the lid.

"Lovely thought Davey."

Inside the case is a laptop computer: "That cash you left me. Thought I'd treat myself. Second hand like. Not going anywhere now, after all." He turns it on and inserts a disc. A vivid green light glares out, illuminating his weathered face, childlike with enthusiasm.

"This is *my* golf course Davey. 'Happy Hills'."

"Ah" I whisper. "I see", I added, seeing nothing.

"Yes my boy. Named it myself. In their honour. They've been good to me, you know. Look."

With the dexterity of a videogame junky, he types a few keys rapidly. Up comes a simulated aerial view of the hazardous hole described in his letter. The green is the size of a postage stamp. "Bob to shoot first" announces an electronic voice. Bob, the friend he'd described in his letter.

"Wicked eh!" says father. *I've only made it as far as 12 so far. 13's a killer! Bob hasn't hit the green in years of trying.*

"Look Davey! Look at the windspeed!"

But I can't look at the screen. My eyes are drawn to the computer itself. Cold, grey, rectangular. Lying before him on the bed. Flat. In the space where dad's legs should have been.

Over the years judges read literally hundreds of twist-ender stories and we can usually spot the "surprise" endings a mile off. There's always something that gives the game away, some small clue. But Happy Hills is that rare gem, a deceptive yarn that manages to present the reader with a genuinely unexpected and shocking denouement.

It's a classic example of how to construct a sting-in-the tail story – a slow build-up of tension, a narrative littered with "misdirection" clues that allow the reader to jump to all the wrong conclusions but which never actually lie to him. It all leads inevitably towards a breath-taking twist in the last ten words. Adam Brown pulls this off with style and perfect timing. Great stuff.

SECTION TWO: POETRY

Convallaria
Convallaria the pharmacopoeia says will strengthen
a heart weakened by years.
by Maura Murphy

Mid-life had claimed us,
restlessness and itchy feet
a symptom.
It was the year my father died
and I spent hours making keepsakes
for relatives I might not see again.

The weather altered, May
became July for a few days.
For a while a truce held,
brought about by finality.

Unsure,
you brought me wild flowers,
Lily of the valley.
Couplets of white beads, open
tender pentagons on slender stalks.
Sheaves of leaves, like bookmarks.

The scent pricked my skin.

So I started drinking to blur edges
of an evening before the funeral.
And I watched our wedding video,
wanting to find my parents,
jitterbugging jiving
on the dance floor of a cheap hotel.

Instead;
I found you,
recognisable, yet removed.
Except for the fraction of a second
on film, when you looked at me.

And I remembered that night,
when confetti fell from us like clothes,
on the stairs, in the bedroom,
off the shoulder falling of a slip.

And of lying awake;
watching threads of a morning
through an old sash window.
Holding a coffee cup,
watching you sleep.

This poem deals with bereavement and also with a difficult relationship, both subjects which have been treated by poets many times before. The approach, however, is fresh and original, and links these two familiar areas in an unexpected but immediately recognisable way. The intense pain at the death of the narrator's father is set against the backdrop of a marriage that's grown stale. The narrator needs to see an image of the parents together on a happy occasion, and turns on the wedding video to see them dancing; only to be entranced by the magic and memories of the day. Although the reader is not told as much directly, we assume that the relationship will be renewed and revitalised by the experience.

*The poem is written in free verse, without any regular pattern of rhyme and metre. But the text is crammed with examples of slant rhyme, where similarity of sound supports and underlines the **feel** of poetry: "May" and "days", "stalks" and "bookmarks", "jitterbugging" and "jiving".*

Its images are compelling. Lily of the valley are described as "Couplets of white beads, open / tender pentagons on slender stalks. / Sheaves of leaves, like bookmarks. / The scent pricked my skin." These lines appeal to the senses of sight, smell and touch, and the bookmark image appeals to the imagination. And all this is done in just four lines.

The vocabulary of this poem is spare, saying a lot with an economy of language, and the construction is finely balanced. Each stanza shifts the emphasis slightly, so that the reader emerges from the poem with a multi-faceted view of the events, characters and subtext of the piece as well as a clear understanding of the circumstances and emotions described.

And But Or
by Charles Evans

I am 'and', simply adding
I'm also, in addition, furthermore
For example: bubble and, mum and, love and
See what I mean? I'm good news, happy afterthought, free gift
And (there I go again) bring you bonuses
In a tacky stick-on-'and'
Of moreness

But I am 'but', checking progress
I restrain, disjoint, modify
For example: everything but, sorry but, love you but
Get the picture? I'm reality, true measurement, sober reflection
And (see first stanza) but your assets.
With a tiny razor-cut-'but'
Of lessness

While I am 'or', changing tack
A choice, another route, fresh options
For example: sink or, your money or, do or
You understand? I'm different, new horizons, possibilities
Or (to coin a phrase) alternivity
By a slender coupling - 'or'
Of otherness

Now don't imagine (from our several voices)
That we are enemies. We work together
To make sense of what you throw at us
You have a complicated world
And it's fascinating
But it's ordered
Or it's chaos

The essence of this poem's success is its simplicity. The poet has taken three common words and considered their meaning and their implications – no more, no less – but has done so with panache and great originality.

Again, the balance of the piece is perfect, with an admirable elegance of construction. Each word is given its own stanza of seven lines, and there is a final seven line stanza that brings everything together. But the pattern of each of the "word" stanzas is satisfyingly similar. A first person voice is indicated in the first line, the second explains the word's significance, the third and fourth give and expand upon examples. The next two lines offer further thoughts about the word, and the last sums it up in two words. The last three lines of the final stanza round the poem off beautifully, beginning with "and" "but" and "or" respectively.

The tautness of the structure is the element that sustains the sense of poetry here, aided by the punctuation which plays a major part in making the poem easy to read and apparently spontaneous. This appearance of spontaneity is usually the result of careful crafting, and it's clear that "And But Or" has been constructed and revised with thoroughness to ensure that it says just enough to engage and satisfy the reader's curiosity, while offering plenty of scope for thinking around the subject it addresses.

Invitation
by Chris Kinsey

If you were here now
what gift would I dare?

Let me unsnake your laces.
Turn your eyes away.

Set your polished shoes aside
to poke tongues at the fire.

Rest your feet in my lap,
give me your soles.

Let my knuckles be
a last for your arch.

My palms want to hold
then mould your heel's dome.

My fingertips will navigate
your peninsular toes

chart ridgeways of tendons
stroke open their valleys.

I'll fan your feet
into wide wings.

Then set you free
to step softer than air.

Again, the originality of this idea is one of its most endearing aspects. In a detailed physical description of the desire to massage somebody's feet, we see a level of focus on this activity and its subtext which is absorbing and resonant.

The poet makes great use of word play. Look at the third stanza. "Polished" means shiny, but it also means refined. This contrasts beautifully with "to poke tongues" which suggests the opposite of refinement, and has a double entendre as a "tongue" is part of a shoe. This play on words is accomplished with ease, and yet there are only eleven words in the stanza.

In the seventh stanza, there is a gorgeous image of the fingertips that will "navigate" sustained by the description of "peninsular toes".

Yet this poem is also a celebration of simple, plain language and its potency. Three of the ten stanzas are constructed entirely from words of one syllable. Three more use mostly monosyllabic words but include a single example of a word of two syllables.

The use of the slant rhyme and occasional full rhymes that are spaced at unexpected intervals create a powerful force holding the poem together. The sound echo produced by "My palms want to hold/then mould your heel's dome" is quite irresistible. The full rhyme of "dare" in the first stanza and "air" in the last gives a beautifully rounded effect.

Pervading the whole poem is a delicate touch – a feeling that the relationship between the characters is fragile and needs careful nurturing. The opening image of a gift and the closing image of freedom add resonance to this idea.

This is another poem that possesses a haunting quality, and lingers in the memory long after it has been read.

SECTION THREE: ARTICLES

HAVANA - THE CUBAN EXPERIENCE
by Leigh Eduardo

So much has been written about the crumbling decadence, the poverty and the third-worldness of Cuba that it is impossible to visit the country without pre-conceived ideas. According to a friend who had recently returned, ¡No hay! (There isn't any!) seemed to be the current in-phrase. This included foods, coffee ... and toilet paper. Determined, I faced the prospect of a somewhat reduced nutritional intake with stoic philosophic abandon: I would turn the tables on deprivation and use the Cuban experience to shed some weight. I also packed a toilet roll!

Surprise, surprise ... the hype far surpassed the reality! While the Cuban cuisine can hardly be classed as adventurous, it was a far cry from ¡No hay! I'm sure there's some truth in the ironic maxim "Tourists first – Cubans last", but I saw little evidence except where luxury goods were involved. Bathroom requisites especially, soap in particular. When delightful older ladies quietly (but most determinedly) approach, requesting ¿Jabón? you soon learn to take the hotel bathroom soap out with you daily! Ecstatic ¡Ahs! came first; profuse thanks immediately followed. It is simultaneously touching and heartwarming – a coupling with which I became very familiar, for the Cubans understand the art of easy communication.

Despite the economic crisis, Cuba is an enormously optimistic country. Nowhere is this more apparent than in the capital. Once

208

accepted as one of the most beautiful cities in the world, I suspect Havana is fast reclaiming that distinction.

The hub of life is centred on the Plaza de la Catedral in the Old Quarter. The square is not large; it could be dropped without trace into most of the Revolution Squares which dominate Cuba's cities and towns. The 16th-century Cathedral has enormous character, watching over the Plaza like a hen guarding its chicks. These particular chicks are the many stall-holders who, since the communist collapse, have been allowed to take on "private enterprise" schemes (largely souvenir stalls) in an effort to aid the economy. Each stall has its own brightly coloured awning so that viewing the Square from the Cathedral steps in the dazzling sunlight presents a feeling of looking into a jewel casket. Here it's possible to buy anything - from string to wooden sculpture, from maracas to a sandwich. It's always busy – an inevitable tourist haunt that somehow never seems touristy.

Also in the Square, one of Havana's most exciting rumba ensembles plays throughout the day at El Patio. Unless you want to splash out around £30 for two for a rather bland meal, just order a refresco and succumb to the fabulous music of the Septeto Sabor playing those famous old rumba warhorses, *El Manisero (The Peanut Vendor)*, or *Siboney*. Like Cuba's mangos, musicians are everywhere. They appear at the chink of a refresco glass, or the click of a fork on a plate. They play; they go. Dance groups set up in the street, perform – apparently for the sheer pleasure of performing - and disappear. No one takes a hat round ... one of the reasons, apart from the superb music and exciting dancing, that visitors give so freely. *Guantanamera* is ubiquitous; it's more of a national anthem than the real thing!

Certainly, there's a fair number of decaying, crumbling once-elegant buildings. But Havana is well into a vast renovation programme, thanks to the World Heritage claim stamped on the city by UNESCO. It's a stimulating if somewhat confusing experience to walk along the winding Malecón, Havana's beautiful sea-front, observing the façades of these once-glorious colonial mansions. A few seem to teeter on the brink of collapse; others, about to be tackled, are surrounded by heavy girders and cranes; quite a number have now acquired a glittering pristine elegance.

From the old walls of the Castillo de los Tres Santos Reyes Magos del Moro (unlike its name, the fort is tiny!) there is a sensational panoramic view of the city. Here, gazing across the Bahia de la Habana, one witnesses a city being reborn. Tall formalistic sky-scrapers vie with 18th and 19th century mansions for domination of the skyline. Then it suddenly dawns that there is no competition; surprisingly, the old and the new actually blend in easy harmony.

There is little evidence of Cuba's Head of State, Fidel Castro ("Fidel" to the people). Far more in evidence, especially in Havana, are tributes to the American writer Ernest Hemingway who lived in the capital for over twenty years. There are statues and plaques in his honour all over the city. His house is now an intriguing museum (shrine?); across the city, many of the writer's old haunts and watering holes still proudly bear his name. There is even a hotel named after his novel, El Viejo y el Mar (The Old Man and the Sea) where I stayed for several nights. Prices were quite reasonable – but even at that level, beyond the average Cuban's income.

If there were extortionate prices for restaurant meals I saw none of them. On the contrary, as a visitor, eating out in Havana can be surprisingly cheap .... and believe it or not, I didn't hear ¡No Hay! once.

This prize-winning travel article is an evocative read, capturing the unusual sights, sounds and side-shows that make up the intoxicating mixture of lifestyles and cultures that is modern Havana. Rather than just a routine description of the city's attractions and tourist haunts, Leigh Eduardo turns his sharp observational skills on to the eccentricities and contradictions of one of the world's most exotic and misunderstood locations.

The anecdote about elderly women asking him for soap tells us much more about life in Havana than several pages of dry facts and figures. So does the fact that street bands come together and play without bothering to pass the hat around. This is a city where people have fun and are happy-go-lucky, even if there are shortages of some basic items.

What also helps to make this article a winner is the author's refreshingly original turn of phrase. When he describes the Cathedral it is "like a hen guarding its chicks. These particular chicks are the many stall-holders ... " and "musicians appear at the click of a fork on a plate".

This is wonderfully colourful writing, rich without being self-indulgent or showy. It creates a spell-binding sense of mood, setting and atmosphere.

It does what all good travel writing should, it lets us taste the special magic of what a holiday destination is like. You can almost imagine you are there as you read. Smashing stuff.

And now, a chance to see how one of the authors of this book fared in competition. He knows the theory but can Iain put it into practice? The unnamed judge's lukewarm comments at the end of this humorous article show that it can take a great effort to impress an adjudicator – even when you're an experienced competitor and know how the system works! See if you agree with his critique.

Video Nasties
by Iain Pattison

WORD went round the building faster than a Christmas Party pregnancy scare. A film crew was coming; we were going to be in the movies! Hollywood fever gripped our newspaper office. Suddenly everyone wanted to be a star.

I tried explaining that the film crew were only a bunch of dozy students from the local polytechnic (sorry, New Age University) coming to shoot a half-hour corporate video, but no-one was listening.

Before you could say: *Frankly my dear, I don't give a damn!* everyone down to the canteen staff had got themselves an agent. It was incredible. Make-up sales at Boots went through the roof – and that was just the men!

It was all the managing director's idea. It had come to him while he was playing with a demonstration video kit in Dixons.

"What we need is something to show we're a paper that cares about its readers. We need – "

"A miracle?" I volunteered.

" – a corporate video. A film to show businesses and schools what we do."

I studied his face for signs that he was jesting. Us? The press gang who couldn't produce a daily newspaper without three nervous breakdowns, two suicides and a punch-up? Go into the movies?

His features were deadly serious. "I've already fixed it," he said conspiratorially, "the media studies students will shoot it for £1,000. You're the managing editor so it'll be your baby. You're going to be my liaison man."

My mouth did Dartford Tunnel impressions. Me? A liaison man? I looked it up in the Hack's Handy Guide to Double-speak. It said: "See schmuck, page 112".

I tried arguing, pleading, feigning death – but I was lumbered. I had this frightening vision of long-haired, vacant-eyed, gum-chewing deadbeats turning the office upside down. Unfortunately, I was right!

Three days later, eight figures shuffled into our front office looking like hippies who'd raided an Oxfam shop. Their hair was greasy enough to fry chips and they exuded a musky aroma guaranteed to send pot-belly pigs mad with desire.

"Where's your tutor?" I asked the nearest outcast from civilization, "he's supposed to be in charge of you rabble."

"I am the tutor," the yeti answered with a hurt sniff. "My name's Taylor, Rick Taylor. You can call me Rick."

I told him my name and ignored the out-stretched hand. "You can call me long distance," I told him frostily.

The next two weeks were a blur of horror. I may have known next to nothing about making a video, but the rabble knew even less.

They filmed with the lens cap on, nearly smashed an editorial computer screen with their tripod, indecently assaulted a passing secretary with their woolly "caterpillar-on-a-stick" boom micro-phone, and spent so long trying to get their arc lights to work properly that tank tops made a comeback.

"It's a bit chaotic, but they've got to figure it out for themselves," Rick enthused, from the middle of a rugby scrum of Best Boys and twisted cable. "This is basically a learning experience."

It was educational, all right! Dumbfounded, I watched as the budding Spielbergs turned our normally cheerful office into a maelstrom of confusion and hate.

Without trying they upset our tweedy deputy editor by calling him Farmer Giles, crashed the classified ads department's computer system, sparked a near walk-out in the press hall and drove the transport manager into a homicidal rage by demanding that the 40 delivery vans be moved to the other end of the compound because "the lights look more sorta atmospheric over there!"

Soon colleagues, who'd been begging to get on screen, were pleading to be excluded. "Who do you have to sleep with to get off this film?" became the office joke.

Things weren't helped by the fact that the female director – a 19-year-old Tartar called Jackie (spelt Jacqui, okay ya?) was big on artistic temperament and hurled non-stop insults at her fellow cinematographers. Not surprisingly, her classmates were a bit put out by this heartless haranguing and day by day the band of film-makers dwindled. It all came to a head on day eight, when her cameraman stormed out after being called a "useless pile of crap" (movie jargon for "less than efficient"). As he exited, letting our only camera fall crunchingly to the floor, Jacqui burst into tears.

"I've lost my Grip," she wailed.

I nodded, solemnly.

We soldiered on, spreading our movie mayhem through the building. I'm not saying we were unpopular, but I've seen drug-crazed burglars get a friendlier welcome.

The film fiends even antagonised one of our biggest advertisers – a local car showroom. It was vital, Jacqui explained, that the video masterpiece should include a section showing one of our advertising reps "out in the field" buttering up a client.

It sounded easy. It would take a few minutes to film. How naïve! Four hours into filming, the crew still hadn't managed to capture a single useable frame.

What they had managed to do was tell the showroom manager that his cars were overpriced, suggest that he change his jacket because it looked awful through the viewfinder and given him a heart attack when one of their lights, mounted on a pole, crashed to earth a millimetre away from a brand new luxury saloon car.

As a seasoned hack I thought I knew more than my fair share of expletives – but my vocabulary was widened immeasurably by the garage boss. Inexplicably, he decided to switch his advertising to our rivals!

Eventually, near the bottom of my valium bottle, we reached the end of the marathon filming session. I was so overjoyed I had to be physically restrained from dancing in the street.

Then everything went quiet – too quiet. Weeks became months, but we had no word of the finished film. Rick Taylor became suspiciously difficult to contact.

In the end I had to go round to the campus and demand to see our epic. After an hour of waffling about dubs, edits, fades and dissolves, shaggy Rick came clean. "It's ... um ... not quite as good as we'd hoped," he said sheepishly.

I demanded a viewing. The results were worse than I could have imagined. By the time they'd edited all the tape that was out of focus, badly lit or covered in soundtrack crackles there was THREE-AND-A-HALF-MINUTES left!

The jumbled, hazy images flashed before my eyes – the way your life does when you're drowning.

It was a disaster. A six-year-old could have done better. I carried the tape back to the MD's office like a timebomb.

He watched in silence, then sighed like a man who's discovered he's won a collection of Barry Manilow records.

"You know," he said, "I reckon a company video is a silly idea. I don't know who thought of it."

Bravely, I didn't remind him. All I said was that it was lucky that we wouldn't now have to hand over the £1,000.

His face went funny. "Oh ... the money. Well, I ... er ... gave it to them in advance."

I cradled my head in my hands.

"They needed it to get a camera," he added, "they didn't have one. Funny that ... "

Judge's comments: This is an amusing and engaging piece. The humour was convincing although it occasionally depended for its force on the deployment of well-worn stereotypes (eg the yeti) rather than by the use of observed characteristics drawn from the scenario itself. This meant that the reader felt that he was "listening in" on the writer's opinions rather than being drawn into a mental world which could be shared with him or her. The piece started and ended well and was, overall, a success.

Hardly bubbling over with enthusiasm, is it? This is one judge who doesn't exactly drown you with praise. But, a win is a win!

Well, did you like the winning items in this chapter? We think you'll agree that they had something that made them stand out, that they were a cut above.

Who knows, after reading this book and trying out some of our suggestions, your next entry might be up there amongst them. We certainly hope so.

And Finally ...

Well, here we are ... at the end. The last pages, the final sign-off. We hope that you've enjoyed our look behind the scenes at the world of competitive writing and found it useful – and entertaining. So drop us a line. E-mail us, care of Writers Bureau. All feedback is welcome. We really do want to hear what you think of the book.

We've tried to cram in as much advice, technique, tips and useful information as we could. We've tried to point out the silly mistakes that most writers make so that you can dodge them and be a prize champ and not a prize chump. We hope it's helped to make you a more focused and more professional player in the game.

And we've aimed to give you the benefit of our experience, not only as judges, but as people who have been mad keen competitors for years. It will be a big thrill for us if our "despatches" from both sides of the battlefield have given you fresh insight and made you think more carefully about what competitions you target, what you write for them and how you submit it.

If you're now a little more ruthless, then our job is done ... Have fun in all your writing, and competing, and we wish you the best of luck. We look forward to seeing your name in that winner's list.

But remember the golden rule – no matter how clever, talented, lyrical and original you may be, you can't win if you don't enter. So don't delay – no more excuses. Get cracking ...

Other work by the authors of this book:

Alison Chisholm

Textbooks:

The Craft of Writing Poetry	Allison and Busby
A Practical Poetry Course	Allison and Busby
How to Write Five Minute Features	Allison and Busby
... and with Brenda Courtie	
How to Write about Yourself	Allison and Busby

Poetry:

The Need for Unicorns	Stride
Paper Birds	Stride
Daring the Slipstream	Headland

As Anthology Editor:

Poet's England: Derbyshire	Headland

Iain Pattison

Books:

Cracking The Short Story Market	Writers Bureau Books

Short Stories:

Iain's short stories have been broadcast on Radio Four, appeared in two creative writing computer program tutorials and have been syndicated in Norway and South Africa.

They have appeared in the following women's magazines:

Chat	Woman's Weekly
Take A Break	Woman
My Weekly	Woman's Own

plus several summer specials and competition anthologies.

Others have been published in:

Acclaim Magazine
Connections Magazine
Writers' Forum